The way to do

The first-ever biography of a Punch & Judy man, *The Way to Do It* explores the life of Frank Edmonds, who worked Weymouth beach for fifty years. His story is told with the colourful collaboration of his family and friends. The book describes what it was like to perform on the sands in all weathers, enduring the rain, the winds and the tight-fisted punters – as well as the golden days of glorious sunshine.

Along the coast from Weymouth, other Punch & Judy men entertained on other Dorset beaches. Every show is different, every showman (or woman) makes his own interpretation of the play. *The Way to Do It* discusses performers and the variety of their performances in neighbouring Swanage, Lyme Regis and West Bay.

Here too is that rare discovery, a transcript of the Edmonds family show, which dates back to Victorian times.

On with the show

THE WAY TO DO IT

Frank Edmonds, Punch & Judy Man

JUDITH STINTON

HARLEQUIN
PRESS

First published in England 2012 by
Harlequin Press
Allshire, East Anstey, Tiverton, EX16 9JG

Copyright Judith Stinton 2012
All rights reserved

Cover design by Mick Orr

ISBN 9780955922411

Printed by Maslands, Tiverton, Devon, UK

Contents

Foreword

Punch comes from Italy, you know.

Frank Edmonds

Pulcinella

The origins of Mr. Punch are a matter of dispute

He's been traced back to Greek and Roman times, his show has been associated with the English mumming plays or given other, more outlandish roots.

What is certain is his connection with the Italian Commedia dell'Arte plays, which date back to the sixteenth century. They were performed by troupes who wandered from place to place, improvising their dramas. There were no written scripts and each actor played one part for life. Among the characters were *Arlecchino, Pedrolino, Pantalone, Colombina* – and *Pulcinella*, who later became Punch. In the plays he was a harsh-tongued, violent fellow, a native of Naples. Like most of the other characters he wore a distinctive black mask and a whitish costume. Pulcinella sometimes had a humped back, he was beaky-nosed and pot-bellied.

When the players travelled farther afield, their names – and sometimes their characters – changed. In France – where Pedrolino became *Pierrot* and Arlecchino, *Arlequin* – Pulcinella's name was *Polichinelle*, and he was often no longer a man, but a string puppet, a marionette.

On reaching Restoration England he at first had many names, shortly anglicised into Punch, which suited him very well. His jester's red and yellow livery suited him well too. Punch became something of a British bulldog, truculent and mouthy. By the end of the eighteenth century for economic reasons he became a glove puppet, and acquired most of his modern accompanying cast.

Not long afterwards, he was taken up by the Edmonds family of Punch & Judy men. Frank Edmonds's father, Harry, his brothers Claude and Walter and his grandfather were all Punchmen, performing in many different parts of the country. Frank Edmonds himself is mainly associated with Weymouth, where he worked on the beach for fifty years.

I devoted several pages to Edmonds in my previous book *Weymouth & Mr. Punch*, (2008), and they attracted a great deal of interest and much fresh information, which has provided the basis of this new book, *The Way to Do It*.

The Way to Do It is, I believe, the first biography of a Punch & Judy man. It describes Frank Edmonds's life as a showman, with contributions from members of his family and from Weymouth people who remember the show. It also contains that rare discovery, a transcript of the Edmonds family play, recalled from the 1960s but dating back to late Victorian times. Many of the illustrations too have not been published before.

Accompanying the script is a glossary of the secret language known as *parlaree* which was used by Punch & Judy and other showmen and which was known to Frank Edmonds. This language derives from Italy, like Punch himself.

Along the coast from Weymouth, other Punch & Judy men entertained on other Dorset beaches. Every show is different, every showman (or woman) makes his own interpretation of the play. *The Way to Do It* discusses performers and the variety of their performances in neighbouring Swanage, Lyme Regis and West Bay.

Above all, perhaps, this book attempts to describe just what it was like to perform on the beach in all weathers, enduring the rain, the winds and the tight-fisted punters, as well as the days of glorious sunshine that are pictured – like Edmonds's show – on many a postcard of Weymouth sands.

Entrances

Working Punch is in my blood.

Frank Edmonds, 1934

2. Frank Edmonds's birth certificate

Frank Edmonds was born on May 11 1903 to a Punch & Judy family, at 4 Victoria Buildings, Lower Bridge Street, Chester. Victoria Buildings was a row of seven back-to-back dwellings, to the rear of a much larger property. Each house consisted of one room downstairs, and two rooms upstairs, there was a single communal tap and toilet, with stables, a midden and a dungheap in the court. Frank was the third surviving child of Henry (Harry) Edmonds, Punch & Judy professor, and his wife Prudence, née Platt.

In later life, Frank often said that his grandfather Andreas was also a Punch professor in London, but we have only his word for this claim. In

3. Victoria Buildings, Lower Bridge Street, Chester

an interview with the *Southern Times* in 1934, Edmonds said that his family had been doing the show for two hundred years. As usual, he was being somewhat extravagant with the truth, and in any case so early a date would not have been possible. His father's birth certificate shows that Harry was born in Holborn, London in 1871 to Andreas Hucké-Edmonds, publisher's clerk, and his second wife Emma.

Frank Edmonds's grandson, another Frank, has done some research on his family's history: 'They appear to live in a fairly well-to-do house in a prosperous area, but by the time of the 1881 Census, Andreas, then known as Andrew Edmonds, is a pauper living in the Strand union workhouse, London, and he is shown as a widower.'

When Harry married at Bilston in 1895, he gave his name only as Henry Edmonds, and, oddly, stated on the marriage certificate that his father was also called Henry, and that he was a musician, who was deceased by the time of the marriage. He gave his own occupation as baker, but in the 1901 Census he stated that he was a 'Punch & Judy showman own account', living at 4 Horsemarket Gardens, Northampton. (He must have been well established by then, as in 1902 he provided twelve Punch & Judy shows for the Coronation route of Edward VII.) Frank Edmonds's Chester birth certificate of 1903 gives his father's profession as 'showman'. Chester was where Harry stayed in the winter, spending twelve of his summers performing in Aberystwyth.

4. Hawarden Castle Entry by Louise Rayner

Frank's grandson notes that Harry's death certificate of August 1939 reverts to his full name, and speculates that because the family fell on hard times 'it may have been possible that Henry was brought up by another relative, who could have been a Punch & Judy man: *musician* might just sound a bit more respectable on your marriage certificate. Punch & Judy men weren't always considered as upstanding members of the community'.

In 1910, Douglas's Directory of Amateur Dramatic Clubs and Professional Entertainers lists 'Edmonds Bros' of 13 Princes Street, Chester under 'Punch & Judy Men'. If this is Harry, as

seems most likely, then it wasn't long before he was moving again.

By 1911, the family were living at 2 Hawarden Castle Entry, a narrow lane between two lines of buildings, off Lower Bridge Street, Chester. The house had six rooms, including the kitchen, and in the Census of 1911 was home to fifteen people, including seven year old Frank. The Entry can be seen in one of the many luminous and intricate local paintings of Louise Rayner (1832–1924), though the 'Row' which crosses it in the painting has been demolished. The Rows are found in the four main streets of Chester and are unique to the city. They are covered passages which run along the buildings at first floor level, with shops and houses behind them.

Frank was Henry's middle child. He had two older sisters, Prudence and Lizzie, and two younger brothers: Claude born in 1907 and Walter, born in 1912. The family also had nine lodgers, who included a knife-grinder, a news vendor, hawkers, haberdashers and an acrobat.

In the Census of 1911, Henry described himself as a photographer, with his wife as his assistant. Like most Punchmen, he could do other jobs. He went to sea as a young man and worked as a ship's cook on sailing ships, still managing to find time to carve his figures. Harry travelled with the show all over the country, and through Austria, Germany, France, Italy, America, Canada and – perhaps during his sailing days – for three years in America, Australia and New Zealand. He performed before Edward VII, a distinction which supposedly entitled the family to carry the Royal Arms on their Punch & Judy booths.

Frank Edmonds always admired his father, regarding him as 'a very good showman … one of the best … I could stand and watch my father's show and laugh and laugh and laugh'. Harry made the young Frank a small show of his own, and he gave backyard performances to the other children, charging them a halfpenny to watch. He told the writer Robert Leach that he began working with his father when he was about ten years old. He bottled for him on engagements which included Aberystwyth and the Isle of Man, where once (so good was he) Harry's booth was set alight by envious Pierrots.

Edmonds also told Leach how during the off-season 'the show was erected in a room over their [furniture] shop, Frank used to slip upstairs at odd times and do a performance of his own. Soon his father allowed him to take charge of an episode in his own show – the boxers first of all, because Frank had developed a good routine with them, then the episode with the Beadle, and so on. When Frank was twelve, his father fell ill at the time of an engagement which he couldn't afford to miss, and this became Frank's first solo performance'.

Although he spent most of his life's summers in Weymouth, Chester was the place to which Frank Edmonds returned, both in winter, and for much

5. *Frank Edmonds's backcloth, used throughout his shows*

of the Second World War. Chester was always literally behind the scenes. The backcloth of his booth was a constant reminder of his origins, showing some of Chester's half-timbered houses and the sturdy Eastgate Clock, erected in 1899 in belated celebration of Queen Victoria's Diamond Jubilee.

6. *The Eastgate, Chester (from the east) circa 1910*

To be a Punch & Judy man, though, he had to leave the city behind. Frank Edmonds ran away from school in 1916 when he was thirteen and a half years old and (as he told the *Southern Times* in 1934) 'took my father's show, without his permission and for six months successfully toured Shropshire and Staffordshire'. This was to be the beginning of his life as a travelling Punch & Judy man, 'on the tober' from February to May and again from September to December. In the summer he worked on the beach; in winter he went home to Chester to perform at Christmas parties. He travelled, he said, all over England and Wales, through parts of Scotland, and to the Channel Islands.

During his ten years on the road he would walk as far as twenty miles a day, pushing his booth on a handcart and sleeping beneath it at night: hard labour, which must have been considerably eased when he bought a five-seater Ford car in which he could carry his booth and sleep.

Frank travelled with a bottler and sometimes with his Dog Toby, who might be given a lift on the handcart. He worked with various teenage friends and split the takings with them. 'I always reckoned a good outside man was worth as much as a good inside man,' he told Robert Leach. Since the bottler was in charge of the takings, it was as well to keep him in the family, and in later years Frank variously used his nephew, his son Frank, his daughter Elsie, his father-in-law, his brother and his grandson as bottlers. This first outside man wore a top hat, and played drum and panpipes to draw the crowd. Tunes played included 'We were Sweethearts' and 'In the Shade of the Old Apple Tree'.

> Punch would join in, singing the words as the crowd gathered, though he had still not made an entry. Then the outside man would conduct a conversation with the invisible Mr. Punch, urging him to hurry up. 'What are you doing?' 'Putting my boots on.' 'Well, what are you doing now?' 'I've forgotten to put my socks on.' And so on. The good outside man is able to orchestrate the audience's response as well as to cover any gaps in the performance: 'Judy, come on, Judy, you're wanted upstairs', while the showman gets Judy onto his hand.

Frank continued to use this leisurely warm-up routine. Weymouth resident Dawn Gould remembered him using a similar technique in the 1930s – doing it all by himself – swazzling to the tunes of 'I'm Forever Blowing Bubbles' and 'Just a Song at Twilight'.

Arriving at a promising spot, Frank would be obliged to seek permission to perform from the police or other local officials. He would ask where – rather than whether – he could give a show, an approach he had learnt from his father. Schools were usually good business. With the head teacher's consent they would put on a performance for the children, charging them 2d each and persuading them to tell their friends and relations that there would be a second show later outside the pub, or on the green. Should this happen, Frank would camp overnight, sleeping wherever he could, in barns, hayricks or under hedges. Any spare cash was spent immediately on food or drink. 'A rolling stone gathers no moss,' he remarked to Leach. 'As you earn a couple of bob, you go and spend it in a pub'.

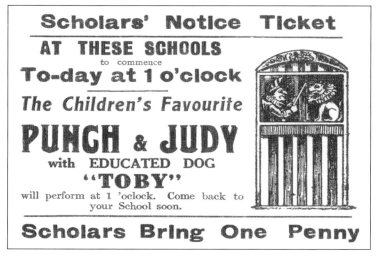

7. Scholars' Notice Ticket, used by Professor Carcass in the 1930s

This way of life (and Edmonds must have been one of the last of the itinerant Punch & Judy men) has left few traces. Little is known about Frank's wanderings in the south and west of England – or of the movements of other Punch & Judy men. Independent, relying on their wits and

8. Itinerant showmen

the gift of the gab, many of them may have been illiterate – though this was not true of Frank, who penned some business-like letters to Gerald Morice, correspondent for the showmen's trade magazine the *World's Fair*. He did not however keep a diary – why would he? Time was away and somewhere else, one day simply following another.

In *Reminiscences of a Showman*, published in 1971, Vic Taylor describes his own working life as a part-time professor, born in 1900 and so a near-contemporary of Frank Edmonds. Many puppeteers were obliged to do extra work to supplement their incomes, but Vic was particularly versatile, working

as a magician, a thought-reader, an illusionist, a hypnotist and a ventriloquist. He was a shoemaker, a trade he learnt from his uncle who was a highly skilled cobbler (and a part-time phrenologist). Vic also served in the Royal Naval Air Service.

For a while, Vic Taylor towed his Punch & Judy show on a trailer behind his bicycle, a 'wild idea' which he soon regretted, especially in hilly districts. He recounts some of his difficulties with bureaucracy, including an incident

9. Vic Taylor

with a policeman who almost arrested him for murder, believing that his ventriloquist's dummy was a human body. The frenetic variety of Taylor's life can be seen from the synopses of his chapters – this example is from Chapter 10. *My second meeting with Captain Kettle [illusionist and magician]; the bottler; I carve a set of Punch & Judy figures; Charlie comes to the fairground; hypnotism with a coloured man; I lose and find Toby; I join the forces again.* (Taylor's Dog Toby went missing on Hayling Island. He found her five miles away, safe in a Havant pub owned by his father-in-law, where she had barked at the door to be let in.)

David Robinson notes in his introduction to the book that 'In Vic's memories, the actual shows and the *mise-en-scène* of Punch & Judy take a distinctly secondary role to all the business of travelling, and lodgings and arranging and being paid. Perhaps this was always so; for in its origins the Punch & Judy show was a make-shift affair'.

When he first arrived in England, Punch, Punchinello or Pollicinella – a few of the many names he has been called – was neither a glove puppet nor partnered by Judy. His appearance was recorded by Samuel Pepys, who watched him in Covent Garden on May 9 1662. 'Signor Bologna' performed what Pepys described as 'an Italian puppet play, that is within the rayles there, which is very pretty, the best that ever I saw, and great resort of gallants'. He witnessed other performances by other puppeteers too, and of the Punch show he said, 'I like the more I see it'. The figure he saw would have been a marionette, worked by strings, and dressed in white. Punch continued as a marionette (apart from some human appearances) while the Punch & Judy show gradually evolved. In the late eighteenth century, however, when he had become unfashionable and down on his luck, Punch assumed the more portable and economical shape of a glove puppet, left the fairs and took to the streets, becoming a *swatchel cove* – a Punch & Judy performer. Two people – one at a pinch – could carry the booth and the set of puppets and assemble a show at a moment's notice.

That said, the *fantoccini* or marionettes (*fantoccini* is sometimes used to refer specifically to trick puppets) did continue to perform, though with different plays. According to Henry Mayhew in his survey of *London Labour and the London Poor*, 1851, they remained a common sight in the mid-nineteenth century. 'Every one who has resided for any time in London must have noticed in the streets a large roomy show upon wheels, about four times as capacious as those used for the performances of Punch & Judy.' The Fantoccini Man's characters, a traditional cast, included an 'enchanted Turk'; an Italian Scaramouch extending his neck; an Indian Juggler; 'the skeleton that falls to pieces, and then becomes whole again'; and 'a representation of Mr. Grimaldi the clown, who does tumbling and posturing, and a comic dance, and so forth, such as trying to catch a butterfly'. This showman regarded himself as superior to his rivals, as his figures were elaborate and costly to make. 'One of them is more expensive than all those in Punch & Judy put together. Talk of Punch knocking the Fantoccini down! Mine's all show; Punch is nothing, and cheap as dirt.'

(It wasn't just Punch & Judy glove puppets which could be dirt-cheap. In his *Everybody's Marionette Book* H. W. Whanslaw zestfully describes how some marionette showmen used to erect 'their rickety "fit-ups" at fairs and other jubilations, when rough-and-tumble dolls, chopped out in the crudest of manners from any old bit of wood that came to hand, with flimsy joints and hideous make-up, jigged and "floated" about, often more in the air than on the stage, when rushlight, penny "dip" and kerosene

10. Candler's Fantoccini

lamps were the only means of illumination'.)

It was much more difficult to work the streets with marionettes than with glove puppets. A good marionette stage is like a miniature theatre in all its parts, more complicated than Punch & Judy's canvas and frame, and therefore far less portable. More puppets are generally used. Punch's street show had a small cast for practical reasons, including such recognisable characters as Judy (who had previously been called Joan), the Policeman, the Doctor and the Hangman. Punch sported his red and yellow fool's motley, and the show would have contained elements of today's perform-ances. Now that they were no longer marionettes, but glove puppets – an older type of doll – they were easier to use, but they had their limitations. As Michael Byrom has observed, Punch, who has become 'paralysed from the waist down…makes up for this disability by possessing a strong pair of shoulders.' Punch was wielding his stick, other characters retaliated and the play became more violent. This was inevitable; fighting is one of the main means of expression for a glove puppet.

The first known Punch & Judy man in England was Giovanni Piccini. In his essay 'A New Light on Piccini', Geoff Felix has suggested that the showman travelled with his brother from Piacenza, leaving an Italy which was 'chaotic and unstable' in about 1779. The brothers would have passed through an equally dangerous, pre-Revolutionary France, and presumably performed along the way, to earn their keep. Piccini settled in London where, according to the Punch & Judy showman interviewed by Mayhew for his survey, he 'used to take very often as much as ten pounds a day, and he used to sit down to his fowls and wine, and the very best of every-thing, like the first gennelman in the land'. But he was careless with his money and performed only when he felt like it, dying in poverty in 1831 at St. Giles's Workhouse off Tottenham Court Road.

For a fuller account of the itinerant life led by a Punch & Judy man like Frank Edmonds in his early days, we have that of Walter Wilkinson, a puppeteer who toured England, Wales and Scotland during the interwar years and beyond, tours which he recalled in his many, popular books.

Wilkinson was by no means a typical showman. As a young man he began by teaming up with his brother Arthur to performing marionette

11. Walter Wilkinson

shows. A devotee of the Arts & Crafts movement from Letchworth, Walter Wilkinson was a rather self-conscious, cerebral performer. He felt that he had been at mercy of the marionettes, by which he claimed he was manipulated, for ten long years. 'And then, finally, I was seized by that gay old villain, Punch. He suddenly insisted that I should become a wandering Punch and Judy man…'

He took to the road with his own version of Punch & Judy, the *Peep Show*, which became the title of his first book. It was a misleading name for the act, as a peepshow is generally a box with a peephole, a 'What the Butler Saw' contraption. But then it could not be called a Punch & Judy show; Wilkinson's Punch & Judy had no Punch, no Judy, no Toby. The original eight glove puppets were an eclectic mix, there was John Barleycorn, his wife Martha, young Pippi, a Pierrot, pretty girl Sally, a Prize Fighter, a Monkey and a Parson. Wilkinson was diffident about his skills, although he was an accomplished puppeteer who could even make a doll plane a piece of wood. He also created some fine figures, and these eight were the first of many (now held by the Pitt-Rivers Museum in Oxford) which included – eventually – Mr. Punch himself. Wilkinson disliked the traditional show, preferring a happy end to the performance. He believed that 'with regard to the Punch & Judy show it is necessary we should have a revolution'.

It was to be an unusually bloodless one, perhaps partly because Wilkinson had been a conscientious objector in the First World War. Yet, despite these artistic oddities (and the sense that he did not really need the cash) Wilkinson in other ways observed the traditions, carving his own puppets from walnut, dressing them, making the handcart and the collapsible booth or fit-up. (Unlike Edmonds he never took to a motor car, a vehicle he despised.) He improvised his scripts and usually bottled for himself, the money soon 'jingling sweetly' in his pockets on more lucrative days. Wilkinson described camping in torrential rain and gales, which happened particularly often one summer in Lancashire. And he encountered officialdom in all its great variety. In Bideford, for example, he was sent by the policeman to the Town Clerk, who directed him to the Mayor (who was also the dentist). The mayor referred him back to the policeman, who sent him back to the Town Clerk to discuss a mutually agreeable rent.

Frank Edmonds's own wandering life ended not long after he married. He met his wife Frances Bailey at Chester Fair, which is held in May each year at the Roodee race course (the smallest and oldest in the country) to coincide with the three-day race meeting. Frank would have been showing for the race-goers as he always found the meetings profitable. The couple were married in 1923 at St. Helen's Church, Witton, in the salt town of Northwick. In 1925 they moved to Lyon House, 23 Watergate Row, in Chester (which is now a furnishings shop). The entry is beside the shop, an ancient building of beams and plasterwork, with a courtyard at the back surrounded on three sides by houses. The couple's first two children, Frank and Ivy, were born in Watergate Row in 1925 and 1926.

As his son Nick and grandson Frank recall, 'Frances never took any interest in the show at all and never assisted him with it. He built the shows, carved all the dolls, made all their dresses, and painted them by himself.' Having a wife and children to support must have been

12.   Frank and Frances Edmonds in later life

the foremost reason why, in 1926, Frank Edmonds took a permanent pitch on the sands in Weymouth. He also took a liking to the town.

Edmonds said that when he arrived in Weymouth he was en route from the Channel Islands, in which case he would have travelled on one of the Great Western Railway ferries which plied between Jersey, Guernsey and Dorset. He had first worked the beach with his father in Aberystwyth and performed too in Colwyn Bay. Though Frank usually claimed that he arrived in the resort in 1926, the Minutes of Weymouth Corporation's Pavilion Garden and Amusement Committee suggest otherwise. When Bert Staddon gave up the pitch in 1924, it was awarded for the 1925 season to a Mr. R. Beavis. In August 1925 it was agreed 'That Mr. Beavis be granted a Beach Site for the Season 1926 for "Punch & Judy" at a rent of £15'. In 1926 Beavis was awarded the pitch for a further three years.

Yet there is evidence that Frank Edmonds was in Weymouth at that time. A postcard of his booth on Weymouth beach is postmarked 1928. In 1931, his daughter Elsie was born in Weymouth, and he would certainly not have moved his family to the town without some sort of security for the future. During the early 1930s the family lived at The Cottage, Dinedors, in Spa Road, Radipole. In *Kelly's Directories* for that period the occupant of the Dinedors house was said to be 'Frederick Bevis Jnr.' Was this a relation of R. Beavis? (The spelling of his name varies from record to record.)

I have previously suggested that Beavis must have been sub-letting to Frank Edmonds. Frank's exuberant successor as Punch & Judy man, Guy Higgins (who was never afraid of a good story), told the following tale in 2004, which he said had been related to him by Edmonds.

> When he first came to Weymouth Edmonds discovered that the Punch & Judy man there at the time was notoriously unreliable, 'largely due to the desire for thoracic lubrication – he liked a drink'. Before the Second World War there were changing tents along the bottom of the sea wall and this man could usually be found in one of two places, the Gloucester Arms or one of the vacant changing

rooms. His booth consisted simply of four bamboo poles, some canvas to go around them, and his dolls.

When a family wanted a show, they would have to ask the beach superintendent to find the Punch & Judy man and he would come to them, set up his booth and do the show. Once paid, he would leave everything where it was, go to the Gloucester and get drunk. At lunchtime closing the now legless performer would be carried on to the sands and dumped in a vacant changing tent, then when another show was required someone found him, retrieved his props from where he had left them and sobered him up.

This was not a satisfactory method of performing, to say the least, and it seems likely that Frank must have taken over the pitch in all but name. Unfortunately, nothing is known about Mr. Beavis and this tale may anyway be apocryphal, a marine myth. In *Reminiscences of a Showman*, Vic Taylor tells a similar story of a drunken performer in Southsea who had to be carried from the pub to his venue. And Leslie Press, son of Percy, has said that in 1948 he had a bottler called Roy Beavis, who was apparently a sober fellow. On the other hand, Frank used to have a doll called Knockabout who was a red-nosed drunk, tartan-clad – could this have been a sly dig at his landlord?

Weymouth Corporation owned the foreshore, and kept a strict eye on the showmen and traders who worked there. The pitches were fixed and numbered; there was only ever one Punch & Judy show on the beach at a time. In this, Weymouth differed from other places like Blackpool, which could have as many as nine booths on the sands. These were secured by a less regulated method, as Robert Leach has described.

Pitches on the beach were obtained by 'scramble' at each outgoing of the tide, showmen wading through the waves to stake their place, and fights over claims were by no means unknown.

There were more orderly procedures for securing the Weymouth pitch, and Punchman Philip Carcass applied in March 1930. The minutes state that 'As Mr. Beavis had written stating it was not his intention to perform at Weymouth this season, Council agreed'. Carcass however did not appear, and in 1931 his application for another Dorset pitch was rejected by Swanage Council (though in 1933 he was appointed as their first official Punch & Judy man). In June 1932, Harry Edmonds, writing from Bridge Street, Chester, had tried in vain for the Swanage pitch, mentioning by way of reference that 'My son has been showing at Weymouth for several seasons'.

More mystifyingly, later that year Harry was granted the Weymouth pitch for 1933. Frank's grandson, Frank, does not believe that Harry ever performed at Weymouth, and an interview with Edmonds in the *Southern Times* in 1934 cautiously states that he 'has held the Punch and Judy rights on the Sands for about four years', which might suggest that he had previously held it in an less official capacity. The explanation for Harry's apparent appearance could be some clerical confusion – as happened occasionally – over the first names or initials of the Edmonds family showmen.

13. Edmonds's booth on Weymouth beach.
The sender of the postcard writes 'You can well imagine the Bairns love Punch & Judy together with the sea.'

By the mid-1930s, however, Frank's position as Weymouth's Punch & Judy man had become established, and was seldom challenged. The fortunes of the Punch & Judy men had changed for the better in the 1870s when they began to move from the streets to the seaside, soon becoming synonymous with the beach. Frank Edmonds, too, took his place at the seaside – he was in Weymouth, he had arrived.

Golden Days: the 1930s

It's almost time for another show.

Frank Edmonds

During the 1930s, Frank Edmonds often ran a dozen shows a day, which he found 'hot work' – especially in a resort with as many sunshine hours as Weymouth, where it was said a doctor 'could neither live nor die'. To keep himself as cool as possible, he wore a bathing costume while performing. All Punch & Judy men work either with their arms at shoulder height or (like Piccini, as George Cruikshank sketched him) with their arms above their heads. Frank preferred the latter. He was left-handed, which made his job more difficult, because Punch traditionally stays on the puppeteer's right arm for most of the show. 'I have to have plenty of practice to keep my arms in proper training, and in the winter, if I haven't any engagements, I have a practice performance. Now I can do anything with either hand equally well and can hold my hands above my head for hours without getting tired', he told the *Southern Times* in 1934. Each of his figures weighed several pounds; Punch weighed in at seven and a half pounds.

14. George Cruikshank's sketch of Piccini in action

15. A characteristic pose,
Claude Edmonds on the right

Edmonds said that 'the only thing I do for my voice is to gargle with salt water when I go for a bathe'. He claimed to smoke 'moderately', but that is not how he is remembered. He was usually seen with a cigarette dangling from his lips; his favoured brand was Gold Flake.

Like most Punch showmen he carved all his own dolls, using willow for minor figures and ash or oak 'for those which have to stand the bulk of the wear'. The dolls' features were made of leather, while Mr. Punch's much-battered nose was made of 'a separate piece of wood jointed in the face' and Jim Crow had an oak leg. Edmonds's brightly coloured figures are distinctive: they have a bold vigour; they look alive.

In the 1934 interview his cast of puppets were said to be Punch, Judy, Baby, the Beadle, Dr. Cratchett – a tiny, bald figure who would 'vibrate like a bell' when Punch hit him – Joey the Clown, the Policeman, the Ghost, Jim Crow, the Executioner and the Devil. Optional extras were the Prize-Fighters, the Crocodile and the Plate-Spinners. Edmonds's theatrical props were the coffin, scaffold, pall, mallet, the punchball on elastic which was used to great effect by Joey, the boxing ring – and Mr. Punch's slapstick.

Edmonds explained that puppets were often handed down through families. He said he had a Punch doll which had belonged to his great-grandfather 'nearly 150 years ago', and which he was now using as a Judy. This statement seems only slightly more convincing than his claim in the same interview that 'there is a clause in the Magna Carta stating "puppets or Punchinella" could perform at any street corner without interference'.

16. *Crocodile, Punch, Baby, Judy, Joey the Clown*

(This does seem to have been a commonly held belief. In 1851 Mayhew's showman insisted that 'Policemen can't interfere with us, we're sanctioned. Punch is exempt out of the Police Act.') Most Punch figures take too much of a bashing to last very long. In the Bethnal Green Museum of Childhood there is a centenarian Punch on display. He looks tired, grey and weedy, he is a miracle of survival. A doll dating from 1785 would be a miracle indeed.

Edmonds always liked to talk of his assured place in a Punch & Judy dynasty. He told the *Southern Times* that as well as his father Harry, his two brothers were working as Punch & Judy men. Claude was a Punchman in Sunderland, Whitby and Filey, and there is evidence that Walter Edmonds performed at Whitby in 1954, perhaps taking over from his brother, who by then had moved to Filey. There is a photograph of Walter with his nephew Sidney, standing in front of Frank Edmonds's booth in the 1950s. Walter's career as a showman seems to have been brief; he worked for many years for John Summers & Sons, a company which had a steel works at Shotton in North Wales, close to Chester.

Frank wore a trilby hat, and kept himself spotless, which must have been difficult sometimes on the sands. He kept his

17. *Policeman, Hangman, Ghost, Devil, Beadle*

Dog Toby spotless too. In the 1930s, as Weymouth-born Dawn Gould remembered, Toby was 'a small long-haired black and white terrier, who looked like a miniature collie'. He sat silently on the playboard throughout most of the show. Training a dog took six months, Frank had used several dogs, and said that this one was the most intelligent, typically billed as an 'educated' Toby. In 1934, his family, which by now consisted of Frank, Frances, and their children Frank, Ivy and Elsie (Sylvia Hazel was born in Weymouth in 1936) were living in Radipole.

18. The Cottage, Spa Road, Radipole

'The Cottage' is still there, a pleasant cream and white chalet with a railway station canopy, which was once a coach house and an apple store. When the family were living in Spa Road it was almost out in the country. Dog Toby, aged four, lived there too, only at home he was known as Psyche (and given a different set of commands domestically). Every day except Sunday, when performances were forbidden, Frank and Toby would catch the bus down the road to Weymouth. On Sundays, while Frank was repairing his puppets, Toby would go on the bus alone to a hotel in Weymouth, where he was given lunch. He seems to have had a good life – though not everyone thought so.

In July 1934, when the writer John Cowper Powys and his companion Phyllis Playter were staying in Dorset, they watched Edmonds's show on Weymouth sands. American-born Playter had never seen a Punch & Judy play before and Powys recorded her reactions on seeing a further performance in September.

She was shocked by the atrocity of a poodle Toby in the Punch & Judy, a living thing among the brutal Inanimates like a girl-prostitute among vicious Rogues. All the little dog's dog-like[ness] atrophied by a process of spiritual Vivisection till he was beyond hope, beyond feeling, beyond caring, and his countenance tricked up like a made-up White Slave 'going through the motions'.

Though some of the audiences for Punch & Judy were beginning to show concern for the welfare of Dog Toby, this was a strikingly early and extreme response (from an animal lover curiously unable to distinguish between a poodle and a terrier.) As Punchman Will Hayward wrote to journalist Gerald Morice in 1955, 'I don't for a moment believe that any but the exceptional buffer [dog] did in fact suffer. All Punch workers of my acquaintance have treated their buffers with the greatest kindness. Anyone in show business knows that only kindness will win the confidence of animals necessary for a smooth performance. Moreover public opinion is strongly against any hint of rough treatment to Dog Toby'. After the War, because of the changes in attitude towards the employment of a live Dog Toby, he was often replaced by a puppet, or removed from the play altogether. Nowadays, it's usually the Crocodile who seizes Punch's nose. In the thirties, though, Toby was a regular feature of the show, perched on the playboard, and leaving it only for the two set pieces: the boxing match and the plate-juggling.

Towards the end of his life, Edmonds described the opening scene with Toby to Robert Leach:

Toby sits on the playboard as the show starts. Punch comes up, dances round singing, and bumps into him.

PUNCH: Oo, oo, my long lost dog Toby, hello, Toby, shake hands, shake hands.

Toby does so, first with one paw, then with the other. Punch then gets Toby to sit up and, using the slapstick, Toby 'shoulders arms'. Punch dances round again, when up comes 'Toby's man' who also bumps into Toby.

TOBY'S MAN: Oo, my long lost Toby, how long have I lost you?

PUNCH: Your Toby? He's my Toby.

He hits Toby's Man with his stick so that he falls flat on the stage. Toby puts his paw out and lifts him up.

When appealed to, the audience always say that the dog belongs to Punch, while Toby continues to follow his Man. A fight ensues between the two would-be owners, Toby joins in and carries Punch off by his large red hooter, much to the audience's glee.

A dog was a definite asset. Although Edmonds was by now a fixture in Weymouth, he continued to do shows elsewhere during the season, including one on a rainy day at Cattistock Races, when people took pity on the sopping wet Toby, offering money even before he had started to perform. Races, from Dorset to Chester, were good money-spinners, while fairs, which historically had been a valuable source of income, became too noisy. Punchmen could not compete with the sounds of hurdy gurdy music, firing from the shooting galleries and excited screaming. Frank's booth in those days was more portable, and could be used for travelling work. A photograph of his fit-up was published in the *News Chronicle* in 1935.

Usually, though, Edmonds worked on the beach. The seaside was where most of the Punch & Judy men could be found in the summer. This pattern had started in the 1870s with the expansion of the railways and the special excursion trains, whose packed carriages supplied the beaches with huge

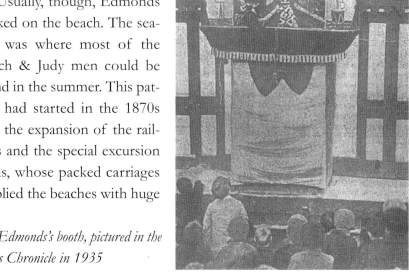

19. Edmonds's booth, pictured in the News Chronicle in 1935

20. Leaving for the Trip

potential audiences. The first week in July must have been as crowded as any in the August high season. This was 'Swindon Week', when employees of the Mechanics' Institution of the Great Western Railway were given free passes to a destination of their choice – and the most popular choice was Weymouth, affectionately known as 'Swindon-by-the-Sea'.

This was no small accolade as, at its height, the 'Trip' offered the railway workers the choice of 350 destinations in the GWR region and beyond (and even abroad). In the 1920s and 1930s over 20,000 people would take a holiday, leaving Swindon almost deserted, while the Company carried out repairs and maintenance of the works.

The first Weymouth trip was in 1870, with a thousand people arriving. By 1936, it was the chosen destination for 5,400 trippers. 'Swindon Week' was unique because of the free passes provided and the variety of the destinations. 'Wakes Weeks', the traditional North of England factory-town holidays – particularly those of the Lancashire cotton workers – were mainly taken in Blackpool.

Both sets of holiday were unpaid, until the Holidays with Pay Act of 1938 which covered a one-week break. Before that, people saved for their holidays through savings clubs, or with their Co-op divi money. The more improvident trippers would spend the return week dodging the landlord when he came for the rent – but usually felt that the holiday had been worth this inconvenience.

The week was a boost for seaside landladies. Most of the holiday-makers brought their own food to be cooked by the landlady in their lodgings – though they were remembered as being famous for the quantities of fish and chips which they consumed. Mr. E. R. Gill's father brought fresh fish from the harbour for his family's breakfast. Like most people the Gills went back to the same lodgings year after year. They went seventeen times to their Wesley Street digs and seemed happy to do so. Others were not so lucky in their choice.

> We used to stay at a boarding house in Brownlow Street, run by a Mrs. C. whose daughter was a teacher at Weymouth Grammar School. We would supply groceries from our rations. Mrs. C. prepared the meals. She spent the afternoons in her beach hut by the sea front. On rainy days she would glower around the front room where guests were making the best of it and say, 'I don't know why you people don't go and enjoy some sea air!'… My parents swapped sides in their bed each night as the uncomfortable mattress rendered sleep on one side very difficult. However, a change of lodgings did not occur to them as Mrs. C. had 'been recommended' by someone at Swindon Works!

This was Stella Taylor, remembering the trip in the 1940s. John Turner had fonder memories:

> Merry-go-rounds, ice creams, donkey rides, sailing ships and steamers, red-coated bandsmen with great silver blowing trumpets, the Salvation Army holding meetings on the sands, Mr. Punch and a vaudeville, lobster teas at Osmington Mills and mechanical toast racks [open buses] that plied their way from the King's Statue to Bowleaze Cove.

Punch & Judy was a part of what historian John K. Walton has called 'the peculiar menu of seaside entertainments, a set of invented traditions with varying pedigrees'. Many of these maritime pleasures could be found in Weymouth, most often on the beach. From the start, Weymouth Corporation, blessed with the patronage of King George III in the early nineteenth century, was quick to realise their resort's potential.

George III was very fond of Weymouth. His personal wheeled bathing machine used to sit on a traffic island there, close to his gilded statue. Although these machines continued to be used they became static, employed for changing rather than for actually entering the water. In the 1930s there were two well segregated pairs of large 'bathing saloons' for men and women and thirty family machines, which, it was claimed, would 'accommodate four people in comfort'. 'Thoroughly cleansed' towels and costumes were supplied and, as a further incentive, tide tables were 'offered free of charge'.

A cheaper alternative was to hire a tent, either a canvas one or the more expensive frame version with wooden floor, roof and locker, which could only be used on the shingle. Neat rows of these tents lined the beach.

By the thirties 'bathing bungalows', some of then two-tiered, could be rented at the Greenhill Terrace end of the Esplanade. These were advertised as being rooms about eight feet square 'partly furnished – *i.e.* table, five chairs, locker, hat and coat hooks, etc. Cold water taps are erected outside'. Even more than personal bathing machines, which were subject to tides, the fixed bungalows had the effect of making that section of the beach feel private. But in other ways, the beach was opening up. Sunbathing was becoming increasingly popular, and costumes were shrinking, though the men still had to wear one-piece bathing suits with a skirt at the front. 'Macintosh bathing' was now tolerated. The visitor would change into his beachwear in his lodgings, covering it with a macintosh on his walk to the beach, thereby avoiding any charges.

Though not always on the same pitch, Frank's booth was then by the statue of the King who had started it all. He was at the centre of the striped shanty town of booths, huts and tents, and close by the open-air beach theatre, known as the Concert Platform. The variety shows of Val Vaux's Vaudesques, and the performances of the pale Pierrots (distant relations of Mr. Punch) must have added to the hubbub. Frank played to enormous crowds, with as least as many adults as children watching his

21. Feeding time

performances. He had no loudspeaker in those days, but relied on his voice.

Like a sandy bazaar, the beach was so crowded that from some spots it was impossible to see the reason for Weymouth's existence – the sea – which was also packed with darting yachts, fishing smacks, warships, pleasure boats and steamers. Ships were tested out in the bay, and giant waves would surge in, leaving the deckchairs awash. There were advance warnings in the local papers, but the visitors were left uninformed and often got wet.

22. Townsend's Merry-go-Round

Donkeys plodded across their stretch of sand, and the wicker goat carts were still in use. Both had been attractions from Victorian times. (One goat cart survived until the 1950s; the donkeys, after a brief break, are still in action.)

Different kinds of rides could be had on the hand-turned 'Juvenile Merry-go-Rounds and Swings', which had been run by the Townsend family since 1918. In the 1930s, Mr. Townsend applied for permission to introduce further attractions such as a Noah's Ark and a Bubble Game. The New Ark lived up to its name – powered by a steam engine, it had fifty-four animals on board. Next door to Townsends was a tent site for hiring out Aquatic Hobby Horses. Bobbing on the waves, the horses provided a mobile frieze for Edmonds's Punch & Judy shows. Next door to his own booth (which was No 20) was that of a palmist called Mrs. Allnutt, who was to restyle herself as a 'character reader'. This must have been a less than happy combination, with hand puppets and hand readers side by side.

There was a glut of refreshment stalls on the beach, including one selling Creamy Whip Freeze Icecream; there was a 'fancy stall', and several photography stands, including a 'While-You- Wait', with a second site on the Nothe. The beach photographers, one of whom had a monkey, are remembered as being rather pushy characters. Also on the Nothe headland was a bandstand; there was another on the Esplanade where military bands used to play.

Entertainments as well as stalls were controlled by the Council, and the Minutes of the Beach Committee reveal how painstaking the work could be – and how troublesome. Visitors were sometimes dissatisfied and even litigious, unofficial beach hawking was a constant problem (leading to prosecutions) as were broken glass and the digging of bait. In July 1935, the mosquitoes on the Esplanade bandstand were so bad that they had to be sprayed with oil of lavender 'prior to and during the performance'. In 1938, beach huts were blown down in a gale.

There was one uniformed beach inspector, Mr. G. S. Nippard, who was well regarded by his employers. He was in charge of the deck chairs which had been introduced in Edwardian days, and of the newer 'comfy' chairs. He presumably had to try and keep order as well.

But business was good, and Weymouth beach was in full swing. In a letter of May 26 1939, Edmonds told Gerald Morice that he had just had the best Easter ever and was expecting a 'record Whit', in what he said was his tenth season. His main concern was for his father Harry, who had fallen very ill – 'the doctors don't give much hope for him'. Harry had retired from outdoor shows, but had been doing a few private engagements.

In a previous letter of February 20, written from his father's house at 6 Castle Street, Chester, Edmonds said that Harry had fifty years experience as a Punch & Judy man. 'I don't think there is a town or village in England he has not shown in, he has travelled most of the countries of the world too'. This almost sounds like an obituary, and in fact Harry Edmonds died six months later, in August 1939. His son Claude inherited his dolls. The only remaining photograph records Harry in front of his caravan, pipe in mouth – trim, smart and ready for action.

Frank was justly proud of his father, and ambitious for himself. In the February letter he asks Gerald Morice to put his name down for a 'Television Broadcast as I give one of the best shows in the country and have one of the best dogs in the business'. After the War, he did indeed make at least one television appearance. But first Edmonds was to receive the royal seal of approval when the King, Queen and little princesses made a visit to

23. Henry (Harry) Edmonds

Weymouth in 1939. On July 22 the *Southern Times* reported rather breath-
lessly on the planned itinerary.

> The Royal family will drive from the station to the flag officers'
> steps opposite the Pavilion Theatre, by way of the Esplanade, and
> the princesses may espy en route the old Punch and Judy show
> which their father stopped to look at as a middy when he once
> landed at Weymouth Pier in the days before the War to catch a
> train for Windsor.

In the following week's edition, after the visit, a 'girl reporter' was
given the task of describing the two princesses and their reaction to
Frank's show. 'Dressed in powder-blue cloth coats and smart matching
tam o'Shanters jauntily pulled on their curly heads', the pair 'made a very
pretty picture as they stepped out of the Royal car'. Princess Margaret
could not resist watching Punch & Judy, while her sister was dutifully shak-
ing hands with Grannie Wallis, 'the town's oldest inhabitant and centenarian'. Excitement mounted as the family sailed out of Weymouth harbour.
'A silent spectator of this extraordinary demonstration of loyalty was Toby,
who sat on the ledge of the Punch and Judy show, watching the scene un-
moved', continued the *Southern Times*.

Since 1936, Frank and his family
had been living at 2 William Street,
where Sylvia had been born. He was
described in that year's *Kelly's Directory* as a 'general dealer'. His dealings
may have been connected with the
shop which his wife Frances kept at
No. 2, a house at the beach end of
the road. (In Frank's version of the
play, Punch's wife has her own business too, a modest 'gin palace' called

24. *The Pig and Carrot (formerly Pig
and Whistle)*

the Pig & Whistle.) Their daughter Elsie remembers Frank using the front window as a space for repairing puppets. He was, his family say, 'an amazing salesman' who could sell you something you didn't really want. He would sell you a bucket with a hole in it, you would take it home and still think you'd got a bargain…

William Street is a short road of small houses behind Weymouth Station, houses which were neither so roomy nor so verdant as The Cottage in Radipole. The street was however much more convenient for the beach, and there was a school on the corner. Yet there was still a problem. 'I had a fairly good Easter', Frank reported to Gerald Morice in June 1940, 'but a poor Whit. I am wondering what to do? for you see since the War I have got a good job here in the Admiralty Service and I get fairly good pay £5 to £7 a week according to the hours I work. I am of course on hush hush business. Normally my season commences at Whit and I can always get more than I am earning now, but will it be my duty to stay at work or carry on with the

Show as usual; what would you do?' His two brothers were already back in Chester, working at a nearby aviation factory 'and they are staying there for the duration or until they are called up'. The 'hush hush business' was probably at Whitehead's Torpedo Works at Ferrybridge on the Portland causeway.

This dilemma resolved itself. In Weymouth 'blacking out' began at the ill-fated and short-lived Pier Bandstand by Brunswick Terrace, which had only been completed in 1939.

25. No 2 William Street (left)

Flags were lowered along the Esplanade. Evacuees had appeared and one of them, a small boy, had smashed a pane of glass in the bandstand. By June 1940 (the date of Edmonds's letter) the Clinton Restaurant was opening from 3pm – 10.30pm as there was 'no business in morning or at lunch'. It closed altogether on July 19. The Alexandra Gardens Theatre was requisitioned, deckchairs were removed (leading to a serious loss of revenue) as was the Concert Platform Vaudeville Theatre. The beach was being stripped – and barricaded. Four foot high blocks were erected at four foot intervals along the sea wall.

In a last desperate attempt to keep beach life going, tenancies and rents were reduced; the charge for the goats and donkeys was cut by 80%. Frank's own reduced rent was written off. But it soon became altogether impossible to trade on the shore.

Frank's son Frank had already taken action. He had left school in 1939 aged 14, and gone to work for the Great Western Railway, sailing aboard the S. S. Roebuck between Weymouth and the Channel Islands. It's thought by his son that he was on this boat at Dunkirk, and shortly afterwards at St.-Valéry-en-Caux, where the vessel was shelled by the German army. Frank's grandson was told that when his father returned home 'my grandmother went ballistic and as he was only fifteen at the time made him leave his job'. (He was to do his war service in the Navy.)

Soon afterwards, Frank Edmonds returned to Chester with his family. As the car door was opened outside their house, Psyche – Toby the wonder dog – jumped out of the vehicle and disappeared. The Edmonds family believed that he had been taken by some soldiers, as there were many stationed in Chester. Toby was never seen again.

Interlude

During the War, Frank Edmonds worked on the degaussing (demagnetising) of ships at Cammell Laird's Birkenhead yard. In the summer season he performed Punch & Judy shows on Aberystwyth beach, which had remained open as it was of no strategic importance.

Edmonds was in Weymouth for the 'Phoney War' period of 1939–40, when all was uneasily calm – except out at sea, that is, where merchant ships were being attacked, and subsequently brought into the Harbour for their protection. When a number of ships had been collected, the convoy was escorted away overnight by naval ships. 'We would wake up one morning and the harbour would be empty', writes Sheila Milton, a former resident of Weymouth. The *Kenfig Pool*, an old cargo ship, blocked the Harbour by night. Scaffolding was erected in the sea, interwoven with barbed wire. The Overcombe end of the beach was mined.

From the beginning of the War, Weymouth's population was increased by evacuees from London, given shelter by local people and overflowing the schools. Sheila Milton remembers how 'some of the mothers could be seen sitting in seats on the prom near Brunswick Terrace breastfeeding their babies. Needless to say shock horror on the part of some of the locals. The poor mums looked fed up and cold'. When the air raids began in July 1940, many of them returned home.

In May 1940, troops of the British Expeditionary Forces (including the Second Battalion of the Dorsetshire Regiment) were trapped in Dunkirk by the German Army. Pleasure boats from Weymouth played a part in their rescue – including the passenger steamers St. Julien and St. Helier. Weymouth was a landing-stage for thousands of refugees. Channel Islanders too fled to the mainland to escape German occupation. Sheila Milton remembers how 'we saw some of the soldiers evacuated from Dunkirk. They were staggering along the prom and the road from the harbour. Some were collapsing on the seats. Their uniforms were torn and some had rifles, some not. They were exhausted. Residents rushed out with cups of tea and buns. It was a shattering sight'.

Weymouth had become a war zone, referred to only as a 'south coast town'. All signs were removed. Even the advertising of Weymouth rock was banned, and its name restricted to its minty centre. By the late summer of 1941 most of the beach was forbidden territory, though an area was reserved for afternoon bathing, which was surely a grey and joyless experience.

After the bombing of Pearl Harbour in 1941, the United States entered the War, and in 1943 more than half a million American soldiers were encamped in Dorset, in preparation for the Allied invasion of Normandy. As D-Day approached on June 5 1944, the roads were full of lorries, jeeps and all kinds of vehicles moving into Weymouth and Portland harbours. The Esplanade was crammed with troops – US soldiers sailing from Weymouth included the war correspondent Ernest Hemingway.

The end of the War was now almost in sight, and with it, the liberation of the beach.

After the War

Where Weymouth Leads

Visitors say that Weymouth possesses the finest Punch and Judy show in the country. It is certainly true that when Punch is doing his stuff there is more noise in the neighbourhood than anywhere else in town, because Mr. F. Edmonds, the man behind the scenes who uses his props with such dexterity, has the happy knack of getting his audience to help with the various problems that arise...If there is a ghost about or such a thing as a crocodile, the youngsters are very vociferous in their warning to poor old Punch. But this is no mere kiddies show, the "excuse" of parents taking their children to see Punch appears to be universally popular.

Weymouth Echo, July 21 1945

26. After the War

27. Hope Street, Weymouth

H e was back.

Preparations for a return to life on the beach had begun as early as 1944, when Weymouth Corporation drew up comprehensive plans for the 1945 season, plans which included a Punch & Judy show 'as heretofore'. In February 1945 Frank Edmonds was offered the pitch again at his pre-war rate of £15 per annum, and in 1946 he was granted the pitch at the same rate for a further three years. (Shrewdly, he managed to keep the payment at this level for many more years.)

The Edmonds' youngest child Nicholas was born in 1947 at The Grange, Hoole Road, Chester. This was a big house, which Edmonds divided up into flats for members of his family. Some of his grandchildren were born there too. The family's Weymouth address was 17 Hope Street, on the water's edge in the Harbour. Edmonds now had five children, and prided himself on his ability to provide for them and his wife from his work as a Punch & Judy man. By 1953 he was staying out at Cerne Villas, a caravan park in Chickerel Road, Charlestown, from where he wrote to Gerald Morice, 'Like my father before me I have worked Punch all my life, since I was 13; that's nearly 40 years ago. I have been married 29 years. I raised a family of five – two boys, three girls – all with Poor Old Punch'.

28. Frank and Nick Edmonds on Weymouth Esplanade

And despite the enforced wartime break, he had definitely not lost his touch.

Vic Banks watched Frank Edmonds perform on Weymouth beach in the late 1940s, when his booth was by the King's Statue. From the age of ten Vic had wanted to be a Punch & Judy man, and Frank encouraged this ambition, showing him the puppets and giving advice. Frank, Vic said, was his main influence and his inspiration. He remembers the show well.

The puppets Edmonds was using at that time were Punch, Judy, Baby, Joey the Clown, Mr. Crow, the Crocodile, the Bogeyman, the Ghost and the Policeman. (Having lost his best Dog Toby, he seems never to have replaced him with a doll.) When he wanted to 'ring the changes' he added the juggling Chinamen (Mr. Punch would interfere noisily in their act) and the two Boxers, who were then Tommy Farr and Joe Louis. Later he brought in the sausage machine. He had Jack Ketch the Hangman among his dolls, but didn't often use him. The Policeman ended up by being hanged instead.

Vic remembered the performance as faithful to its Victorian origins in the Edmonds family, and remarked that it was rather like a Pierrot show, all-singing and all-dancing. Mr. Crow would provide music with drum and tambourine. Frank was a fine artist, one who stood up to perform rather than remaining seated: this produced a much more flowing movement during the chases around the proscenium. His puppets had loose hands, which would move as they crossed the stage to exit, theatrically. They did not just drop down out of sight as is often the case. Edmonds was an expert swazzler too and Punch's voice rang out very clearly. While some Punch & Judy men would have other characters echoing Punch's words Edmonds did not need to do this, as the audience could immediately understand what had been said.

His was a virtuoso performance. The Bogeyman had a big nose, which Punch twirled about his rounded stick. The Chinese Plate-Spinners provided another display of skill. It was also a show which appealed to children. The puppets really whacked one another, and if they fell against the slapstick there was a loud bang.

Edmonds used rabbit fur for the dolls' hair. The Crocodile had a fringe which swayed as it moved, to comical or frightening effect, according to the audience's response. The Baby was thrown out on the end of a cord, and could be hauled back in under the playboard, like a child controlled by reins. The body of the unfortunate Policeman, who had been tricked into his own execution, was put in a coffin, his face washed with spit and prayers said over his body. Then the Clown carried the coffin around the stage in unsteady triumph. Everyone ended up dead, except Punch and Joey. Joey then whacked Punch, and suddenly all somehow seemed well again.

Money was collected in a box on a pole, which made it easier to reach those standing on the prom. Skilled trader though he was, Frank didn't sell any souvenirs. In the same way, he never gave himself the honorary title of 'Professor'. His approach was very straightforward. His play was a 'running show' with no change of scenery – the Chester Town Clock remained imperturbably in the background. 'It was a Punch & Judy show and that was it.'

Vic Banks added that Frank Edmonds used to give interviews to the BBC and to the newspapers, and that he had once been the castaway on *Desert Island Discs*. Although not a man to waste words, Frank enjoyed talking and actively courted publicity, perhaps increasingly, as more opportunities arose in the post-war years. The Punch & Judy show was now much less likely to be dismissed or disregarded in the press, and had at last been included as a feature in the official town guide – along with the donkeys.

In January 1947 Gerald Morice reported in the *World's Fair* (journal for Punch & Judy men, circus performers, slot machine vendors and other itinerant artists and traders) that he had received a letter from Edmonds containing a cutting about his latest venture: 'Weymouth's "Uncle Frank" did a month's engagement with Punch at Messrs Plummer Roddis at Yeovil.' (There was another such store in St. Mary Street, Weymouth, trading as 'ladies' fashion specialities, General and fancy drapery, soft furnishings, ladies' outfitters, costumiers, etc.') Edmonds had performed four shows a day at Yeovil's Plummer Roddis, mainly to full houses. Broadcasts from the show could be heard on December 7 and 8.

In his letter, Edmonds added that Muirhead Bone (actually his son Stephen, with whom Bone went on painting trips to the seaside from his cottage near Lymington) had produced 'his impressions of and response to South Dorset's unequalled scenery [which] have been recorded in several pictures'. Some of these pictures by Stephen Bone were on display at the Leicester Galleries, London, including 'Punch at Weymouth', which was reproduced in the *Listener* magazine on December 12 1946. It features Frank's booth on the beach among a scattering of deckchairs which face the sea. Leaning against the booth, with his back to the show, is a flat-capped figure holding a mug of tea. Unless this was a pure invention, like the Swanage fiddler described in a later chapter, the figure must have been the bottler, who after the War was his brother Claude's son Sidney. His family are adamant that Frank always wore a trilby hat.

Stephen Bone (1904–1958) who like his father had been a war artist, was one of the many who celebrated Englishness in the early post-war years, recording a world which had so nearly been lost. In 1956, Bone contributed a book called *British Weather* to the 'Britain in Pictures' series, which covered all manner of subjects from porcelain to sea fisheries to rebels and reformers. (A similar series for children, Picture Puffins, had an acting edition of Punch & Judy by Clarke Hutton.)

Confirming that Punch & Judy was now established as a part of the English tradition, showmen Percy Press (the 'Amusing Amazer') and Swanage's own Ernest Brisbane were among the attractions in the Festival of Britain, 1951. They appeared in the Festival Pleasure Gardens in

29. Punch at Weymouth by Stephen Bone, 1946

Battersea Park, amid 'the flowers and the lakes and the fountains'. Sponsored by Sharp's Kreemy Toffee, the stage had an illuminated tree and multi-coloured fairy-lights. This event took place one hundred years after the Great Exhibition at Crystal Palace.

The Festival's own exhibition was made up of a series of pavilions on the South Bank, telling a 'continuous story' of the British Isles. The seaside pavilion was schematically divided into three sections: the seaside at work, the sea coast, and the seaside at play. The latter included a rock stall because – as the rather lavish guide explained – this pepperminty confection was a feature of the unique 'equipment' of the seaside.

> …every single stick of rock contains an ancient mystery. On the top of each of these pink and white sugar cylinders is inscribed the name of a particular seaside town. You bite the top off the rock; you bite on and on to the sticky end – but at each stage the lettering remains embedded in what is left of the rock. How the letters get inside, and how they go all the way with you, is a question which has puzzled most people since their childhood. The answer can be found in a stall in the Seaside Section where you can see how this miracle is manufactured.

Come to the Festival Pleasure Gardens—come to the flowers and the lakes and the fountains—come to the Fun House, the Grotto, the Miniature Zoo—come to the bands and illuminations—come to the eating and drinking and dancing—come to the shops, the theatres, the fireworks!

Open: weekdays 10.30 a.m. to 11.30 p.m. admission 2s. (children 1s.) Sundays 12.30 p.m. to 10 p.m. admission 1s. (children 6d) by train, underground, bus and water-bus from the South Bank Exhibition and all parts of London.

30. Poster for the Festival Pleasure Gardens, 1951

All this bright and breezy business with magic rock and funny hats and period peepshows, is conducted here against a background of a characteristically British "seafront"; a medley of Victorian boarding houses, elegant bow-fronted Regency façades, ice-cream parlours, pubs, and the full and friendly gaudiness of the amusement park.

'Rock' is here described at greater length than 'rock pools', an unexpected touch of frivolity in an exhibition which had a serious educational purpose. Seaside pleasures, it would seem, had become a respectable part of life.

The beach looked somewhat different after the War. Gone from Weymouth were the bathing machines, the Pierrots and the Concert Platform. The musician Edward Page, in his book remembering his childhood in the resort in the 1950s, gives a boy's eye view of those summer sands – the deckchairs, the sand in the sandwiches, sunbathing and the resulting 'pink lobster effect', the beach trays, candy floss, Punch & Judy and the donkeys. His gang of boys went down to the beach with their tennis rackets, which were used not to play games, but to sift the sands for loose, lost coins. Abandoned bottles drained of their dandelion & burdock or ice cream soda (products of South Dorset Trades) were duly returned for the deposit money.

The boys discovered that Punch & Judy too could be watched for free. The sight of the collecting box was their 'cue to leave quietly'. As well as the regular characters, Page remembered seeing 'one puppet, playing a well-to-do drunk dressed in top hat and tails, [who] would sing a topical song of the day in his inebriated state. The song …went something along the lines of 'I've seen lights and diamonds again, hic, hic'. This was probably gleaned from the local revellers at pub closing time'. Frank's scruffy, tartan Knockabout of the thirties had gone up in the world, though his drinking habits remained unchanged.

Adults as well as children had very little money in the early fifties, a time of austerity, with rationing still in place. Edward Page describes his parents' harbourside boarding house at 19 Trinity Road, where 'holiday-makers' had the luxury of a rickety indoor glory hole of a bathroom. This facility was 'a small room, about the size of a small hotel lift, with the outside tacked and covered with corrugated iron', suspended about twenty-five feet above the ground. The alternative was an outdoor lavatory at the bottom of the garden, equipped with a roll of 'sharp-edged, tough, crinkly, Izal, prison-issue toilet paper' attached to the green door, with a paraffin lamp – and 'mammoth' spiders.

No one seemed to mind this discomfort. They were simply glad to be on holiday and, like the Swindon trippers, ready to return regardless to the same lodgings, again and again. Their clothes, too, reflected their financial state. Edward Page describes how a typical holiday-making couple would look: 'He in a forties sartorial, uniquely made, one-size-fits-all demob suit, his best Sunday, interview, funeral suit and holiday posh wear given to him as he left the forces in 1945, she … in her aquamarine-coloured hand-knitted twin set and pearls.'

While on holiday, most people liked to look smart. Dress rules had to be observed on the beach, and there was still a beach inspector to ensure their observation – but not without some anomalies. A photograph by the Revd. Edward Tanner of nearby Preston shows Frank's booth with his usual surrounding hordes – beside the massive sand sculpture of a reclining Marilyn Monroe, curves nicely in place. This was in 1957, when the wearing of bikinis was forbidden on the beach.

31. Frank Edmonds' show, with an added attraction

Weymouth's sand is a pure limestone, ground by the movement of the tides into a fine powder. It is ideal for making sculptures – and also for the sandcastles which daily decorate the beach in a few brief hours. Sandcastle competitions were a major attraction during the early twentieth century, inspiring some highly ambitious creations. Commercial sponsors of competitions included the makers of Bovril and the Daily Mail newspaper.

Not long afterwards, the sand modellers arrived. Some of their works were one-dimensional, pancake-flat, like the work of pavement artists. Others were sculptural. Part of the appeal for all of the modellers was that the only materials they required were sand and sea water (a pint of

32. Edwardian sand pictures

water to two pounds of sand) both immediately and freely available from the beach. By the 1920s there were so many artists that the Council felt obliged to regulate them.

One of the sand artists was Fred Darrington. Born in Weymouth in 1910, like Edward Page he spent much of his childhood on the beach. He and his brothers began by drawing on the sand. In 1983, speaking of his life, he said: 'There were forty or fifty of us young lads who used to be down there making the models to show the visitors, hoping for a few pence for our efforts. Somehow, my models were always a bit more on the grand scale. And I'd go to a shade more trouble than most. For in-stance, I'd make a model of a house, then I'd push a bit of burnt rag inside and the smoke would curl up out of the chimney'. He taught himself; he had no formal training.

Unimpressed – and suspecting that money was being made – the Council kept moving the boys on. Then Fred was given his own pitch, and there he stayed. At first the Council stipulated that his models were built below the high water mark, which meant that they were washed away at every tide. Sand sculptures are by their very nature transient, returning to the beach from which they came, but such a rapid disappearance must have been very discouraging. In the 1920s and 1930s the tide used to flow right up to the Esplanade, until new breakwaters were built in the bay. Eventually, the Council (as well as the tides) became more accommodating; it would 'even send a JCB at each end of the season to move the sand'.

Even so, the sculptures only lasted a matter of weeks, a brevity which did not bother Fred. For him, the pleasure was in the making of them. Later he discovered that he could prolong their brief lives by coating them in poster paint. His nephew Michael, aged ten, wanted to take a model of a monkey home with him in the boot of the family car, but it fell apart on the journey home. Monkeys were a favourite theme: in the 1930s, Fred had a pet monkey called Jenny, which he used to take to the beach with him. 'Fred got into a bit of trouble with Weymouth Council on occasions, because the monkey was a bit naughty: at one point she stole towels from a hotel, and frequently bit my auntie Betty', says Michael Darrington.

Fred's subjects varied from an enormous tableau of the Last Supper to monkeys playing poker, or from the Prince and Princess of Wales to a scene from the Falklands War. Of the latter, he said 'There was a flag in that Falklands tableau. I kept seeing it out of the corner of my eye and thinking "Hello, who's flying a flag on the beach then?" It had that silky sheen, it was furled and creased just right. It took me in time and again'. He was so good, he even fooled himself.

Fred spent long hours on the sands, just as he had as a boy. He had a small hut

33. Fred Darrington and friend

(roofless to begin with) where he could eat his lunch or wash his hands, he used to keep a mynah bird in there, which he taught to talk. Mainly though, he could be found in his fenced-off space up against the Esplanade, working, with his back to his constant and often vocal audience. He raked the ground for coins and also displayed a musical bucket, which clanged when a giver aimed accurately, hitting the bottom. A notice beside it explained his technique, in verse:

> *The secret of my recipe is water. paint and sand.*
> *A simple knife a little patience and a steady hand.*

Fred Darrington taught these techniques to Michael, who spent a summer season as his apprentice, he also taught his grandson Mark Anderson, who has the Weymouth pitch today. Before 1962, Fred worked on the sands in the summer and in the winter was an electrical engineer. By then, like Frank's, his fame reached beyond Weymouth. He gave interviews and demonstrations and once did a sculpture of Goldie, the Blue Peter labrador, with sand transported specially from Weymouth to the BBC Television Centre. Modestly, Fred gave all credit to the Weymouth sand. He said 'It's perfect. There's no other like it in the world'.

34. Fred Darrington at work

35. The finished sculpture

Fred Darrington and Frank Edmonds were great friends, Frank was also friendly with Fred's mother and father; they all used to go to the races together on their days off. Fred's mother owned a fancy goods shop in St. Mary Street, quite close to Frank's booth, 'so tea and chat were exchanged in between working', as Michael Darrington remembers.

After World War Two another 'sandcastle man' was Jack Hayward, celebrated for his intricate sculptures of cathedrals. In 1947, the Council discovered that he was modelling without official permission. He immediately offered to cooperate, by paying rent at a rate of £20 pa. When this sum was raised to £25 in the following year he protested, claiming that he was 'at the free end of the beach'. The Council promptly retorted that there was no such thing but, after a legal wrangle, Hayward succeeded in avoiding the rise. He remained on the beach throughout the 1950s. In 1963, when Jack Hayward was in hospital, Fred Darrington took over his pitch.

The sand sculptures are on display at the harbour end of the beach. When Revd. Tanner took his photograph of Frank's booth flanked by a siliceous Monroe, Edmonds's pitch was close by, next to the Lost Children's area. Edmonds's earliest known predecessor, Professor James Murray, would sometimes perform beside the Jubilee Clock, on the island built to curb the ever-encroaching shingle from covering the sands.

However the King's Statue pitch was (and is) the most common site for the booth. Vic Banks suggested that Frank perhaps moved southwards because it was quieter – further from the Pier Bandstand where, due to the shortage of suitable players, the military bands had been replaced by 'more colourful civilian bands'. The musicians on the pier fascinated Edward Page, with their 'gravy-stained, thirties dinner suits' and 'openly secreted' bottles of whisky. They played 'bland evergreen standards'; later, they tried unsuccessfully to update their repertoire with Elvis Presley numbers, incongruously delivered on clarinet, trombone and tambourine.

The services on the beach were just as noisy and rather too close for comfort. Page remembered the bonneted ladies of the Salvation Army cheerfully singing hymns to the accompaniment of a 'sand-filled harmonium, which seemed to sink further and further into the sands as its player vigorously pumped away'. Neighbouring St. John's Church held services there, as did the Ebenezer and Bethany Hall, the Open Air Mission and other religious organisations. A huge mound of sand was used as a platform, with pictures on the front, made from flowers. Other meetings clogged up the Esplanade. However, Frank would seldom have been forced to put up with them as – a sore

Beach and Clock, Weymouth.

36. James Murray performing by the Jubilee Clock

point – they usually gathered on Sundays, when he, despite his best efforts, was not allowed to perform on the beach.

It was not for want of trying. In 1946, on Edmonds's behalf, the secretary of the Amalgamated Engineering Union requested that the Council rescind their resolution not to allow Punch & Judy on the beach on Sundays. The Council refused. In 1951, Edmonds was told that he could give shows on the Sabbath between 4pm and 7.30pm (while Townsends were allowed to operate their children's roundabout between 2.30pm and 8.30pm). Frank's allotted hours would have coincided with the services. In September 1957 he applied for permission to start earlier on Sunday afternoons, a request which was referred to the Beach & Entertainments Committee 'in view of the controversial nature of this question'. At the November meeting the matter was deferred for enquiry 'of the Religious Bodies who might be affected by any decision' in the matter. Then, rather perversely, in January 1958 the Committee agreed that as religious services could be held on the beach on Sunday afternoons, then so could Punch & Judy shows. Edmonds was allowed to start at 2.30pm, but could not use his amplifier until 4pm. It was several more years before he was allowed to perform on Sunday mornings.

The amplifier had already caused trouble. As the *Echo* had reported in 1946 'It is certainly true that when Punch is doing his stuff there is more noise in the neighbourhood than anywhere else in town'. By 1949 Edmonds had an amplifier to swell this sound, and Mr. John Carey Talbot of Talbot & Read ('chartered auctioneers, estate agents and valuers') who had offices opposite King's Statue at 10 Royal Terrace, complained about the noise and demanded that the booth be moved to a site further north. The Council played for time until the following year, when representatives visited Talbot's offices and as a result agreed to move the Punch & Judy pitch. A further outcome was that the Council received a solicitor's letter on behalf of Mr. S. H. Mulley, who claimed that he had rented his refreshment stall by King's Statue because of the proximity of Punch & Judy – and that his trade would be 'seriously reduced' with its removal. The Council then agreed that 'the Punch & Judy show be returned to its original site and that the proprietor be requested either to cease using an amplifier in connection with his performances or very much reduce its volume'. It seems unlikely that Edmonds complied with this request other than temporarily; he had won the round.

So it was perhaps not by choice that Frank found himself next door to the Lost Children's wooden hut. On approximately the same site there had been an 'Excursionists' Day Nursery'. This was founded by the ex-nurse mother of the writer Rosemary Manning (several of whose books are set in Weymouth) in the Edwardian period, when the family lived at 2 Gloucester Row on the Esplanade. Rosemary Manning describes her mother's enterprise in her memoir *A Corridor of Mirrors*.

> At Weymouth, she had conceived and carried out a piece of social work original for its time. Every summer, swarms of 'trippers' descended upon the town. In those days they spent their brief holidays in boarding houses, where it was the custom to turn them out after breakfast and not admit them again until the evening. Young couples dragged their small children along the esplanade and across the sands, often in sweltering heat or sometimes in pouring rain. My mother set up a day nursery on the beach, where families could leave their babies and toddlers all day for a trifling

37. The Day Nursery on Weymouth Sands

sum. There she and her helpers fed them and cared for them while their parents were set free to enjoy themselves.

Frank's core audience was of course children, though, as photographs show, he was still managing to draw in many adult spectators as well. A family man, he was fond of small children and his kindness is often recalled. From her 1930s childhood Silvia Noakes remembered that Edmonds stored his booth and props in a garage at the New Cooper's Arms in Maiden Street. When he repaired his puppets, she would sit on his knee 'and he would practise his various voices'. She enjoyed having a Punch & Judy show 'all to herself'.

Frank encouraged the young Vic Banks in his ambition to become a Punch & Judy man. He allowed Dawn Gould, a Weymouth child whose mother ran the bathing machines and taught swimming, to make friends with his Dog Toby. From the mid-1950s Fred Hawkins remembers how Frank had a caravan in the summer, in the middle of the miniature railway which was then by Radipole Lake, with the track looping around his caravan. On summer evenings he would sit on the steps as the boys played around the site. He would give them a drink and chat to them. Frank's years of performing meant that he knew how to make the boys laugh. Sometimes he would go off for a pint at his local, the Rock Hotel in Abbotsbury Road, which he reached via a lane.

This site, Frank's grandson recalls, 'was owned by the Council, the people who lived there were all seasonal workers, mostly fairground,

38. Frank's grandson by the Lost Children's hut

and a few beach people like us. I think he only paid a few pounds to park there for the summer season, the Council came round and emptied the chemical toilets once a week. The only other thing you got was a brass key for the one tap we all shared. We washed, shaved, and cleaned our teeth in cold water, using an old enamel bowl and wash stand. Sunday morning we all went to a laundry in the town for a hot bath, whether we needed one or not. Breakfast was boiled eggs every day; lunch, though, did vary a bit. One day it would be Canadian Cheddar cheese sandwiches, and the next day it would be ham sandwiches, and then back to the cheese again. Not having a fridge, fresh food was bought almost daily, when we had a cup of tea it was always with tinned milk – Carnation probably'.

Fred Hawkins, who looked after the advertising hoardings on the prom, also remembered another man in a trilby – Lobby Lud. He was the figure-head of a competition invented by the *Westminster Gazette* in 1927, the name Lobby Lud coming from the paper's telegraphic address, which was 'Lobby Ludgate'. There were various takeovers of the newspaper, which ultimately became the *Daily Mail*. Lobby Lud was a mystery man (only his silhouette was pictured in the *Mail*) dressed in a suit, with a trilby hat and pipe. Edward Page, another fan, described him as resembling 'the comic detective character Sexton Blake, the Prince of the penny dreadfuls'. Mr. Lud carried a copy of the latest edition of the newspaper under his arm. The paper contained an announcement of the resort in which he might be spotted. If found, he was to be approached with the words 'You are Lobby Lud and I claim my five pounds'. All this was especially fascinating to children though, sadly, competitors had to be over twenty-one to make a claim.

Frank Edmonds, famous, but not familiar, as he was usually hidden in the narrow confines of his booth, would have been advised to leave off his hat when he walked out on the prom. Five pounds was a lot of money in the 1950s, and there would have been many eager seekers after this ingenious prize.

The War had gone, but was not forgotten. Swiftly, in 1945, defence works had been demolished on the Sands and Esplanade. The Alexandra Gardens Theatre and other buildings were de-requisitioned; the rolls of

39. Lobby Lud, as seen in the Westminster Gazette

barbed wire were removed. But memories lingered longer. A. J. Liebling, a journalist on the *New Yorker*, revisited Weymouth in 1959, on a 'sentimental journey' to the places he had known at D-Day. Standing on the Esplanade, he watched part of the Punch & Judy show. He was too late for Judy, but in time for Joey, to whom he took a strong dislike, nicknaming him 'Smarmy'. In his book *Normandy Revisited* he describes the performance. The only feature of the show he admired was the audience, the crowd of blonde children – 'not Angles, but Angels', he wrote, quoting St. Gregory.

> The smarmy puppet said to Punch "'Old out your 'and, I won't hurt you." He held a sledge hammer behind his back. Punch shrieked apprehensively and waved his hands about his head. Smarmy appealed to the angels. "I won't 'urt 'im, will I children?" he asked them. "No!" they all shouted in chorus, following with an explosion of knowing squeals. Poor Punch wavered. He appealed to his little friends in turn. "Will 'e 'urt me if I put my 'and out, children?" "No!" followed by more squeals. "All right pal. 'Ere's my 'and." He extended his right hand, palm up. Smarmy hit it with the sledge hammer. Punch screamed realistically, and the angels howled so hard with laughter that mummies and nannies had to drag half of them away to public lavatories.

40. Frank talking to Punch, Joey Edmonds on the left

This alien and condescending account does at least provide a record of the extent of audience participation the performance now involved, a recent phenomenon influenced by pantomime and, later, by television. The Punch & Judy show was continuing to evolve. Involving the audience was a way of doing it.

41. Left to right: Frank Edmonds, his father-in-law Tom Bailey and his son Frank

Swanage:
Dreams and Nightmares

I have met a few of the pros including Smith of Margate, Stafford of Exeter, the Codmans of Liverpool, Green of Rhyl, old Maggs late of Bournemouth, young Staddon of Boscombe and a few more.

Frank Edmonds to Gerald Morice, 1939

Like seaside snow, Punch & Judy was a rare sight in Swanage for years. While Weymouth had a resident puppeteer from 1880 or even before, Swanage Urban District Council was slower to accept what it plainly regarded as a humble form of entertainment.

In 1904 Professor T. Day of Hastings had brazenly set up his booth on Swanage beach without any official permission. His proud claim that his show was 'Patronised by Royalty' was one which failed to impress the Council, who ordered him to 'cease his performances in the town'. On September 10th, the *Swanage & Wareham Guardian* reported on the unpopularity of this decision.

> A good deal of comment is made upon the action of the "powers that be" in stopping the Punch and Judy show from performing near the gardens each night, where it has been a great source of attraction both to old and young, and certainly doing no harm or causing annoyance to anyone. We quite agree that our town is greatly appreciated by the visitors for its quietness and relief from nigger troupes, &c., but we believe if a census were taken of the visitors and residents a very large proportion would be in favour of the Punch and Judy show to remain undisturbed. No doubt at the Council meeting next Monday we shall hear more about the matter.

On September 17th it was reported that when the Council debated the matter, Mr. John Woodford White, Swanage estate agent, demanded 'If you are going to allow Punch and Judy, where are you going to draw the line?' The barrow owners complained that 'they had to move on every few minutes, while the Council allowed a Punch and Judy to remain and collect a crowd'. White said it had been a 'misapprehension on the part of the Inspector' to permit the performances. When it came to the vote, the majority of Council members agreed with Mr. White.

Professor Day responded with a petition signed by both resident taxpayers and visitors from London, which the Council simply ignored. Yet a Punch & Judy show – as brilliantly coloured and raucous as a stray macaw – would not have seemed out of place on Swanage beach. The town had already attracted more than its share of oddities and incongruities, in the shape of statues, false frontages and metropolitan gaslights.

42. Professor Day on Swanage beach

The artist Paul Nash, who lived in Swanage from 1934–5 (during which time he wrote the original *Dorset Shell Guide*) was very much taken by the place, and the architectural bric-a-brac was a major part of its appeal to him. In his essay 'Swanage, or Seaside Surrealism', Nash imagines how a ship-wrecked stranger might struggle through the wild waters to the safety of the Swanage shore. When the waves begin to draw him back, 'he clutches desperately at a lamp-post. The refuge saves him, and, as he sinks forward, his eye falls on the embossed letters round the base. The fitful light momentarily throws up the silver-painted words: "St. George's, Hanover Square".'

There were several of these gaslights on the front, each showing England's patron saint battling with the dragon. (Two others on the Durlston Estate were marked 'Grosvenor Place' and 'Northumberland Avenue'.) They had been put there by local entrepreneur George Burt in the mid-nineteenth century, architecturally salvaged from London, along with a clockless clock tower, 'grey and papery against the solid sea', some bollards and a 'façade of bad but genuine design [by a pupil of Christopher Wren] grafted onto the late nineteenth century Town Hall'.

In 1862 Burt's relative and rival, John Mowlem, who built the now-demolished Institute, imported a stone column, 'surmounted by a pyramid of cannon-balls set askew' which commemorated Alfred's defeat by the Danes in the bay. This remains a feature of the Esplanade, the only one of a welter of imported monuments which has any direct relevance to Swanage.

Nash, who also liked the chalk landscapes, the white-faced cliffs and downs, delighted in Swanage's 'strange individuality' which came with its metamorphosis from fishing village with stone boats to a respectable watering-place of an endearing ugliness. It had, he believed, like all things surreal, 'the power to disquiet'. Nash's watercolour 'Swanage 1936', is a gathering of sticks, stones and upright bones, a dreamy seascape with threatening figures, poised as if for some sinister beach performance. His was a peculiarly home-grown Surrealism, set in identifiable surroundings and incorporating objects which (as Alexandra Harris has noted) were often familiar enough to be 'native to any English antique shop'.

During his stay in Swanage, Nash sketched, painted, and took photographs with his Kodak camera. Serving in Flanders in the Great War, he had been gassed; he suffered badly from asthma and this sometimes made exploration difficult. Photographs could – and did – serve as a starting-point for future work, and this kind of record could highlight different relationships between the objects being photographed than those seen by the naked eye. Objects were Nash's subject. He wrote 'I don't care for human nature except sublimated or as puppets, monsters, masses formally related to Nature'. Swanage, with its ironmongery, beachcombings – and sublime landscapes – was to remain a feature of Nash's work for several years afterwards.

Meanwhile, the Urban District Council was also coming to realise the full potential of the beach. This had taken time. In 1926 it had rejected the application of a man who is now regarded as one of the finest Punch & Judy operators, John Stafford of Trowbridge (1902–1981) who became Paignton's Punch & Judy man until 1969. Like Frank Edmonds, he featured a live Dog Toby and a virtuoso boxing match. Like Edmonds too, and other performers of the period, he had an act which was more comic than violent, perhaps because he so much sympathised with his leading doll, saying 'When I'm in that show I am Punch.' His Punch was likeable, a kind of hero, able to laugh at his own considerable frailties. 'My Council do not permit entertainments on the beach at Swanage,' wrote the Clerk, oblivious of the strengths of Stafford's show. Three months later Moore's Wonderful Living Marionettes – Dolls that Sing and Dance in 'Lilliput Follies' – were also refused permission to perform, despite their owner's claims that they were 'absolutely clean, refined and free from any vulgarity.' 'Clean' in this context, meaning wholesome, was a word which acquired more sinister connotations with the rise of the Nazi Party. It was an adjective used with approval in the twenties and early thirties, but was not enough to earn the Marionettes a place on Swanage beach.

In 1931 the Clerk also responded grudgingly to an approach by Philip Carcass, one of the Brighton Punch & Judy family. They insisted on references in spite of his well-established reputation. Not surprisingly, Carcass replied rather huffily.

> Dear Sir,
> Yours forwarded I am on Tour. I am surprised you require references, I am about the oldest performer now living, 67 years of

43. Swanage 1936 by Paul Nash

age. Performed all my life Punch and Judy. I perform the usual, about 4 Shows per day, one in the morning, about two [in the] afternoon and one about 7o/c Eve, only in fine weather…

His response came with a file of papers – references from Liverpool, Torquay and Newton Abbott, a photograph of his booth, and a newspaper report on the death of his Dog Toby in Paignton, during their annual appearance in that seaside town. Toby, a Yorkshire terrier, aged thirteen years and two months, was a 'great little actor' of some fame. 'No more than four times in its dozen years of activity, did this Toby delight and arouse the admiration of Royalty, and, in the winter time, when there were no little children to entertain on the beaches, the terrier made a round of the "halls" in all parts of the country.' Endorsing this claim, Carcass's headed notepaper had a weighty list of patrons, including the King and Queen. He may have performed all over the country – but this was not as yet to include the little town of Swanage.

44. Puppets made by Swanage puppeteer, Ernest Brisbane

In 1932 there were at least three hopeful applicants for the job, the first being Gus Wood of Hampstead, whose cast of characters included Joey, the 'Clown Proprietor of Oil and Meat Store'; Uncle Joe, a Jamaican; Master Marwood, the Executioner; and Nobody's, the Ghost. Gus Wood lived from 1912–1962; his dolls are now one of the splendours of Bethnal Green Museum. From a plain proscenium, with classical columns, marbled in pale green, his Punch & Judy figures gaze unsmilingly at the visitors, while the Ghost lurks in the shadows behind them. Wood's puppets have been described by Robert Leach as being 'comparatively crude and child-ish' with 'the aura of a child's nightmare'. Undeniably, they are rather grim – this is an unpleased Punch, like Piccini's in Cruikshank's cartoons. Even Joey the Clown, peeping out at the back from the booth's skirts in a red and orange, grey and white costume, is looking rather thoughtful. Around the booth Wood's props are arranged: drum and panpipes, frying pan and a collapsing Jim Crow, the coffin and the pall, the gallows and a rolling-pin. It must have been quite a performance.

The second applicant in 1932 was P. Coleman of London, who enclosed a photograph of his booth, and who had been in Teignmouth during the previous season. His Punch & Judy was, he wrote, like Moore's Marionettes:

'clean and free from vulgarity'. This does not seem much of a recommendation: such a show would be like fish and chips without the vinegar.

The third applicant was Frank Edmonds's father, Henry. As we have seen, Harry was a showman of great experience, but his offer, like the others (and all three were notable performers) was turned down. Yet in the same period the Council was allowing a bagpipe player, Mr. F. Glover of Swanage, to perform seasonally on the beach, despite some spirited protests from visitors about the noise. The sands were apparently bare of any entertainment other than the shrilling of the bagpipes, and Mrs. Staddon's lonely pony toiling up and down the shore.

Then, all at once, in 1933 Philip Carcass was allowed to perform, at a charge of 30/- a week, and was given a pitch 'near the Mowlem Institute'. The Council's stance was changing. Soon it was allowing not only a Punch

45. *Application from Philip Carcass, with photo of booth and his famous Toby*

& Judy show, but also a beach photographer and the sale of Wall's Ice-cream.

Successful performers still had to contend with Clause 5 of the Council's contract which stipulated that; 'Neither you nor any person employed or authorised by you shall obstruct, annoy or molest the members of the public frequenting or using the beach where your site is situated, and shall

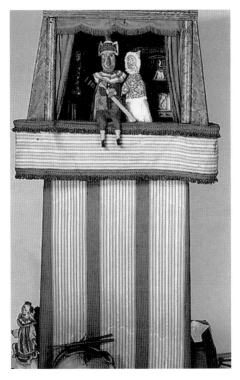

46. Gus Wood's Punch and Judy

not shout, blow any horn or ring a bell, but shall behave in a quiet, orderly and respectable manner.' Enforced, this rule would have been the kiss of death to any Punch & Judy puppeteer.

The next showman to be granted the pitch was Percy Press in 1935. He performed magic, ventriloquism and Punch & Judy up to five times a day for seventeen weeks in the Amusement Park facing the beach. It was his first season as a Punch & Judy man, but records are unfortunately hazy at this point – the Council was deeply absorbed in buying the foreshore, and in comparing its tariffs with those of other seaside towns, such as Herne Bay and Teignmouth. Swanage Council was becoming less strait-laced – although the delights of the 'Whoopee Bathing Floats', which were tendered in 1936, were adjudged as being beyond the bounds of good taste. (Here they were missing a trick: Whoopee Floats were already netting a tidy sum for Weymouth Council.)

Late in 1937, Ernest Brisbane of Hornsey was offered a pitch close to the first shelter on the Esplanade, but wrote to say he would 'using Concert Platform at Westcliff' for the 1938 season. After the War, in 1946, he put in another tender but was too late, as the pitch had already been let to Bern Hastings. Brisbane's time in Swanage was yet to come.

In April 1940 Bern's brother Joe Hastings enquired about the site for Punch & Judy and 'ventriloquial entertainment'. He was asked to offer for the season – including Sundays. In May he agreed to a spot opposite the Amusement Park for £7 10/- a six-day week, excluding Sundays. (With

47. P. Coleman's booth

hindsight, this proved a fortunate concession, as the Council then received a letter from a Miss E. M. Langford 'together with a petition signed by a large number of residents' whose objections to Sunday performances could well have proved insurmountable in those stricter days.)

Joe Hastings was the puppeteer who worked as technical advisor to Tony Hancock on his film *The Punch and Judy Man* in 1962. Hancock had spent much of his childhood in Bournemouth, where his parents ran a hotel and where he would have seen a Punch & Judy man on the beach, most probably one from the Staddon or Maggs families. Philip Oakes, who co-wrote the script with Hancock, wrote that 'the film was largely based on his childhood memories of Bournemouth and, whatever its shortcomings, does have the tang of salty, chapped nostalgia which comes close to our original intentions'.

Along with his Bournemouth links, Hancock had a Swanage connection. For two years after his father's death in 1936, he attended Durlston Court School, overlooking the bay. His performances in the school plays were unremarkable; he excelled himself on the playing fields. His first major success as a performer was to be with another doll – he acted with Archie Andrews, a ventriloquist's dummy operated by Peter Brough. 'Educating Archie' was that odd thing, a radio show starring a ventriloquist and his dummy. Archie was a truculent schoolboy, educated at home because no school would accept him. Among other parts Hancock played his tutor, and he intensely disliked his squeaky pupil. This was something of an ill omen for his later film role with Mr. Punch.

In his account of the film-making, Philip Oakes observed that it was

48. Harry Edmonds's application

not a happy period in Hancock's life. Like Punch, and like his character in the film, he was quarrelling bitterly with his wife, who 'gave as good as she got'. He was also frightened by the puppets, especially the bloodthirsty Crocodile, and seemed afraid of swallowing the swazzle, the metal instrument which, when concealed in the mouth, produces Punch's squawk. When Joe Hastings explained this trade secret to him, adding that he was quite likely to swallow a few of them, Hancock remained sceptical. He blamed Punch for everything that went wrong: he was 'the embodiment of old evil, the libido, the malevolent mocker'. He was sure that the film was jinxed – a fear confirmed by Hastings's death from lung cancer just before it was released. (This did not stop Hancock from sending a floral Punch tribute to Joe's funeral: a Punch complete with stick, made with red carnations.)

In the end, though he worked the puppets, Joe Hastings became too ill to swazzle. Percy Press, who was doing the summer season on Hastings Pier, received a phone call from the studio asking him to dub the soundtrack of *The Punch & Judy Man*, an action which Press neatly described as 'post-syncopation' in a letter to Gerald Morice in 1962.

Like someone in a haunted house, during the making of the film Hancock jumped at every turn. He was so much on edge that he took fright when he was given a 'Slinky', a coiled steel spring which could 'flip-flop' down the stairs 'with a life of its own'. Failing to destroy this scary object, Hancock took it to the beach one night and buried it in the sand.

Hancock's reactions were extreme, but not unique. It is not only small children who fear Mr. Punch. In M. R. James's 'The Story of a Disappearance and an Appearance', published in *More Ghost Stories of an Antiquary*, the unnamed narrator is spending his Christmas in the country, helping to search for his uncle Henry who has mysteriously disappeared. The year is 1837. There have been Punch & Judy men in the district and on Christmas Eve the narrator has a dream about the unseen show. He finds himself in darkness waiting for a performance to begin. After 'an enormous single toll of a bell' the curtain flies open and the show begins.

49. Tony Hancock, Archie Andrews and Peter Brough

There was something Satanic about the hero. He varied his methods of attack: for some of his victims he lay in wait, and to see his horrible face – it was yellowish white, I may remark – peering round the wings made me think of the Vampyre in Fuseli's foul sketch… But with all of them I came to dread the moment of death. The crack of the stick on their skulls, which in the ordinary way delights me, had here a crushing sound as if the bone was giving way, and the victims quivered and kicked as they lay.

This is a savage, murderous Punch – no slapstick here, no accidental deaths – who meets his match with the horrible, revengeful appearance of murdered Uncle Henry. There is nothing juvenile about this show.

Cheerier, child-centred shows were by now in place at Swanage. Joe Hastings's brother Bern was on the beach in 1946, after Joe had turned down

50. Hancock and Mr. Punch

an offer of the pitch. He wanted to provide a children's roundabout and ventriloquism as well as Punch & Judy, and this had not been allowed.

Bern Hastings tendered again in 1947 and was offered the Mowlem Institute site. (He applied twice more in the late 1950s in the guise of 'Professor Chad'.) Oddly enough, Frank Edmonds, writing from 17 Hope Square, Weymouth, applied in 1947, when the Council's charge was £50 – considerably more than he was paying for his usual pitch. In 1950 Frank Bolden, also known as "Dezot" (or Dizzy), clown-conjurer and Punch & Judy man of London NW1, put in a tender. He was yet another excellent Punch & Judy man, and a very clear swazzler, who took his teeth out to perform. Bolden, perhaps unwisely, explained that he had been at Shoeburyness for the past two seasons 'but it has not payed, so now desire a better position'. He offered £15, because, he said, he would need to hire a collector and find lodgings. He pointed out that he had only been charged six guineas by Southend Corporation. The Council agreed to his offer, recommending a site south of Victoria Avenue. But two months later Mr. F. E. Bolden had found other work.

There seems to have been a Punch-less beach in 1953 as well. Freddy Beale of Bournemouth (who'd applied in 1939) offered £10 for sixteen seven-day weeks, 16th May–13th September, excluding Coronation week. He refused to pay the requested rate of £30, and so the Urban District Council agreed to a £16 fee. Days before he was due to start, however, Freddy Beale withdrew. From 1954-56 the Punch & Judy man was Syd Downe of Kingston, Surrey – who also complained about the charges.

Then Ernest Brisbane of Hornsey (real name Fred Scudder) offered to perform 'a series of Punch & Judy performances' from mid-May to mid-September, 1957, 'from a structure measuring 4'10" x 4'6" to be erected for the season'. He tendered £25, which was accepted. Brisbane moved to the neighbouring hill-village of Langton Matravers into a house called Lynford in The Hyde, just below the Kings Arms inn. David Saville, who lived next door to Lynford and bought Brisbane's car when he left, still remembers him. He was a tiny, dapper man, very quiet and polite, with a wife who 'kept herself to herself'. They were a private pair, who didn't attend church or join in any activities. Brisbane was known by younger villagers as 'Arthur Askey' after the famous music hall star.

Brisbane had been one of the Punch & Judy performers at the Festival of Britain in 1951. It was here that he first used the 'sausage machine', a gruesome device which turned the Baby into bangers. (He's been credited too with introducing the 'Spider' routine, later used to great effect by Weymouth's Guy Higgins.) Brisbane stated that he was a 'Gold Star Medallist of the Inner Magic Circle', a conjurer, ventriloquist and games organiser as well as Punch & Judy man.

He also proved to be a demanding performer. First of all, he asked for permission to sell 'photocards of his outfit' to his audiences on the beach, a modest request to which the Council agreed. One of the photocards showed him in 'Brisbane's Children's Corner' with his live Dog Toby. (A later photograph shows him standing trimly in front of his booth on Swanage sands with a puppet Toby on his arm.)

Brisbane then asked for reimbursement of the cost of removing and repositioning his show from a pitch previously approved by the Council 'in view of complaints of obstruction of view by occupiers of two beach bungalows'. They did not object to his show, he claimed, but to 'folk standing on the promenade' to watch it.

The Council prevaricated, requiring more details of the matter. Brisbane went on to request the concession for the next three years at £20 per season. The Council agreed to £25 for 1958. Brisbane countered this by submitting his expenses of £2 19/- and asking for an early decision on the next year's site. (He was given one opposite the Information Bureau, now the Tourist Information Centre.) Brisbane was not very happy about his existing site as 'the Spring Tides cause lots of worry and expense'. The Council eventually agreed to refund his removal costs.

Ernest Brisbane got the 1959 concession for a site 'near the slipway and shelter off the bottom of Victoria Avenue'. In August of that year

51. Brisbane's Children's Corner

he complained about this pitch, which had 'proved very unsatisfactory from the income point of view' and asked for another site 'just north of the ice-cream kiosk near the Amusement Park as the promenade at that point was much wider and there would be ample room for pedestrians to pass without stepping on the roadway'. The Council insisted that the existing site was acceptable, and offered it to him for 1960 at the same price. Brisbane, 'disappointed', then asked if he could advertise on the Ice Cream Stations at the ends of the Promenade. The Council refused.

Having been granted the 1961 concession, Brisbane requested the 1962 one for the same price, but with a reduction in the event of a further show being provided on a nearby private beach. He said that he had been approached by the Proprietor of the Ocean Bay Hotel, a man who threatened to put in a rival if Brisbane did not agree to perform in front of his property.

The private beach lies at the eastern end of the bay, bordered by bathing huts and bristling with notices reminding passers-by of its selectivity. At the western limit there are four tall 'Private Parasols', stiff with thatch in a rustic Caribbean style, worthy of the camera eye of Paul Nash. Despite all the fuss, it does not seem that any Punch & Judy performances ever took place on this part of the beach.

When Brisbane asked again about notice boards – which he said would be much tidier than the current fly-posting – and for permission to sell 'puppet cloth models of Mr. Punch', the Council continued to refuse, despite Brisbane's insistence on the matter. It seems to have been a tricky year for both parties, but there was one consolation. 1962 was the year in which Brisbane's

52. Private Parasols

Punch & Judy show was painted by local artist Percival Arthur Wise. In the picture an expansive booth stretches along the beach in the golden glow of a summer's afternoon. The sea is blue and calm, the audience intense and still. Punch and Judy are in action, but the most energetic movements come from a bearded fiddler, in breeches, accompanying the performance. This imaginary creature steals the show.

In 1963 Ernest Brisbane announced he would be 'leaving the country' in January 1964 and asked if he could sell his equipment at the end of the season – in fact he took the dolls with him to Wellington, New Zealand, where he and his wife planned to make a home with their 'very happily married' only daughter Iris and her family. He continued to perform Punch & Judy shows as well as ventriloquism and magic. His granddaughter Margaret Wyllie remembers seeing his swazzles soaking in a glass of water (like false teeth), then drying on the kitchen window-ledge after performances. In 1943 a swazzle had nearly killed him. While he was performing at the Alexandra Palace, Brisbane was found unconscious, his puppets beside him. He was believed to have swallowed his 'squeaker', and was rushed to hospital.

Brisbane's puppets have recently been auctioned and returned to England. His scripts (and notes) accompanied his puppets. Brisbane relied on written plays; his sources included *The Story of Punch* by Fred Tickner, Edwin Hooper's *Hello Mr. Punch* and the anonymous *Description and Dialogue for giving a complete Performance of the Famous "Punch & Judy"*.

Tipped off by Brisbane, Mr. Herbert E. ('Jock') Armitage applied for the 1964 season, on the usual terms. Originally from Glasgow, he was a gentleman's hairdresser by trade, working in London for many years before moving to Swanage, where he had a business at

53. Ernest Brisbane in Swanage

54. Punch and Judy on Swanage Beach, Dorset by Percival Arthur Wise

38 High Street. In London he had become acquainted with Ernest Brisbane as they lived in the same neighbourhood for twenty-five years and 'knew each other as residents and entertainers'. Armitage inherited both Brisbane's booth and his site at the bottom of Victoria Avenue. A versatile performer, Armitage belonged to the Puppet and Model Theatre Guild, he was a magician, and a member of the Bristol Circus Ring. On becoming Swanage's Punch & Judy man he moved to Flat 7, Steepway, Peveril Road – and, presumably, gave up his hairdressing business.

Armitage followed in Brisbane's path. In 1968 he managed to beat the rent down to £10 by hinting that he was 'considering' applying to a cheaper place. He pointed out that in Brighton the fee was only £5, 'including 24 deckchairs and free storage', and that such a rate was not unusual.

Jock Armitage was the subject of a picture book called *Punch and Jonathan* with text and photographs by Bill Binzen, published in England in 1970. 'Uncle Jock' is first glimpsed, dressed in a clown's costume, striking a gong to draw attention to the show. He is standing outside the booth – now looking more battered – which once belonged to Ernest Brisbane.

55. Cover photograph for Punch and Jonathan

His Punch is a saturnine presence; his face is as dark and disdainful as the last Shah of Persia's. He overawes Judy, a little doll with a heart-shaped face. When one evening Punch escapes from the bag of puppets, a boy called Jonathan finds him in the road and takes him home for the night. Jonathan now has the chance to do what he has always dreamed of doing whenever he watched the show. Early the next morning he gives his own performance on the cliffs, to an audience of curious cows. Here Jock finds him and, impressed by the show, appoints Jonathan as his apprentice.

The puppets featured in Binzen's book are a striking set of dolls. Jock Armitage was also photographed around the same time with another, very different Punch & Judy couple, a boozy-looking pair with wine-red cheeks and noses.

Uncle Jock left Swanage in 1974 and went back to Glasgow to live in the house in which he was born and where he was to die. He was succeeded by Paul Gold (one of whose talents was fire-eating) to whom he left his magic props and his Punch & Judy. A contemporary postcard shows Paul Gold using a live dog, just as Brisbane had done in his early days. Once in Swanage, Gold (also known as Paul Bruce)

56. Jock Armitage

began by requesting an electricity supply for his booth 'by means of an overhead cable from the Ice Cream Kiosk', to be used with what he re-assuringly called his 'small ampli-fier'. The modern world was encroaching like an insidious tide.

When Gold retired to Spain in 1976 his pitch was taken by Wendy Wharam, one of the very few fe-male Punch & Judy (or Judy & Punch) operators. A feminist, with an indomitable Judy, Wendy had a grudging respect for Punch and his anarchic ways. In her show, Punch did not kill Judy, and was repri-manded by the bottler for his vio-lence. Her approach was quite a

57. Paul Gold

change, and an innovation for Swanage Council – but one that was not to last. On December 5th 1990, the *Purbeck Independent* reported that the Council was refusing permission for Wharam and her partner Peter Jaggard to rent the pitch for the 1991 season. The Council was complaining about the increase in the charge to see the show and about noise levels. It also alleged that in one performance a Mrs. Thatcher puppet had been hanged by Mr. Punch. The performers defended themselves, saying that 'Mrs. Thatcher was, in fact, eaten by a crocodile', and that the episode had happened five years before, never to be repeated.

Swanage had moved a long way from the bagpipes and Mrs. Staddon's lonely pony.

58. Wendy Wharam

Puppets on a String

One of the tunes Frank Edmonds played on his controversial loud-speaker was the 1960s hit 'Puppet on a String', sung by the appropriately named – and bare-footed – Sandie Shaw. It was an apt choice.

Frank had been using string puppets in his show during the 1950s. From childhood he had known how to work the marionettes, which he had himself done 'occasionally' as he told Gerald Morice in a letter of 1939. 'As regards information on marionettes, I think my father would be able to give you some, as he spent all his life touring the country with one or the other'. In a further letter of 1940, he asked if he could borrow 'a book or two' on the subject. And in 1946 he still had marionettes in mind as part of his postwar plans. 'I have decided to train my son Frank who has been demobbed out of the Navy to work marionettes and also of course 'Punch'.'

If Edmonds did borrow books from Morice, then one of them would have been H. W. Whanslaw's influential *Everybody's Marionette Book* published in 1935, which covers almost every aspect of the complex art of making, setting and performing with string puppets.

The methods for making the puppets had changed little over the years. Most were carved out of wood, just as Punch and Judy heads were made. The bodies of marionettes required a lot more work than those of glove puppets, because they had to be shaped before being dressed. They were complete figures, not just heads and hands. As an authority on the subject, Whanslaw goes into great (and essential) detail on how to do it: detail which also exposes the main differences between the two types of doll.

Speaking heads have to be able to open and close their mouths convincingly, a tricky business, as their facial movements must synchronise with the voice of the speaker. Eyes are concave and often without pupils. The shadow cast by the upper lid when the puppet is in motion 'does really suggest a lot of movement', Whanslaw wrote. Eyebrows always have to be dark, or they will disappear under the lights.

Marionettes' bodies used to be made out of linen or wash leather, stuffed with bran or sawdust, which left them prey to rats and mice. Now, more durable materials are used. All major dolls are jointed at the waist, and how their joints are made depends on what they are intended to do: there are several choices.

Not only do marionettes have waists, they have legs and feet as well. Many a Mr. Punch – including Frank's – has legs and feet, and so does Frank's Mr. Crow, but these puppets tend to flop and dangle in their dancing. The working legs of marionettes bring their own problems. When they move, the upper part of the puppet's body is likely to swing forward as well. To correct this two small discs of lead, the size of an old penny, are nailed to each side of the lower body section. The upper arms are weighted too.

The jointing of the neck, elbows, knees, wrists and ankles is also crucial to the production of convincing movement, and close attention has to be paid to the carving of hands and feet. Sometimes the soles of the feet are weighted too. This is all a delicate balancing trick – and afterwards the puppets still need to be strung and attached to horizontal controls.

The booths are different as well. At its simplest (in the form of a portable fit-up) the Punch & Judy booth is a three or four sided frame, covered in canvas, with an opening near the top for the proscenium. The marionette booth, on the other hand, is generally more complex. Frank's pre-war booths could not have been used for string puppet performances because they were covered by cloth. Only in the 1940s did he have a wooden booth, which gradually became larger and more elaborate. Later booths were hinged about half way between the playboard and the ground, so that the proscenium could be lowered for use as a marionette theatre. Frank would then be operating from above, instead of from below with arms raised as he did with Punch & Judy. There does not appear to have been any scenery in his plays – a black velvet curtain behind the puppets served to conceal both the puppeteer and the marionette strings.

In one way, though, marionette performances had become easier. Gone were the candles and the smoking oil lamps of the old-time showman. Now there was electricity, which both removed the danger of fire

59. Edmonds's booth, with electric cable connected to the neighbouring stall

and allowed the stage to be lit more brilliantly and more effectively.

Edmonds soon had an electricity supply, as his grandson Frank describes.

> '… Not only did he have electricity, but he had free electricity and as many cups of tea as he could drink … a cable was connected to a nearby stall selling tea, candy floss and sticks of rock. They obviously knew they were on to a good thing having the stall right next door. Occasionally there would be a complaint about the cost, he would threaten to move to another part of the beach, and no more was said.'

Edmonds mentioned his interest in marionettes in several letters, and his family recalled that he used them at some point after the War. His grandson remembers playing with them as a child, 'especially the skeleton. I would usually end up with all the strings in a knot, which the more you tried to entangle just got worse. He would eventually see the mess I had got it in and end up cutting all the strings, and re-stringing it.' But the only visual evidence of his string puppet show is the photograph, belonging to Frank's great-nephew and Claude's grandson, Keith Ellis, which shows Sid Edmonds and Frank's other brother Walter watching a marionette performance. Sid Edmonds is sporting a quiff, which suggests that the photograph was taken at some time in the mid-fifties.

The three marionettes on the little stage are the 'Dissecting Skeleton', Grimaldi the Clown and the Indian Juggler. All three of these dolls date back to Victorian times at least, and were used by Mayhew's Fantoccini Man in *London Labour and the London Poor*. All three feature in Whanslaw's book as 'Trick Dolls': the 'traditional' skeleton and the clown 'of a Grimaldi type' are two of the figures which could come to pieces and join

60. Frank Edmonds's marionette show, watched by Sid (left) and Walter Edmonds

together again. The Dissecting Skeleton would climb out of a coffin in a graveyard, dance itself to pieces, re-assemble, and drop back into its box. The Grimaldi figure in Whanslaw's drawing looks very like Edmonds's Clown, with his cocked hat, breeches and cheery grin. Immensely popular,

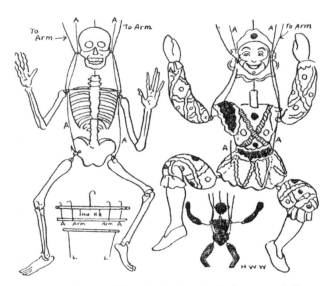

61. H. W. Whanslaw's sketch of dissecting dolls

Grimaldi (1778–1837) performed all over the country – including shows at his father-in-law Richard Hughes's Theatre Royal in Augusta Place, Weymouth. He was skilled as an acrobat, and claimed by the end of his life to have broken every bone in his body during his stage career, which made him a fitting subject for a 'dissecting' doll.

The Indian Juggler too was based on an actual person, a performer called Ramo Samee (his real name was probably Ramaswamy) who lived in England from about 1819 until his death in 1851. He was said to be England's first modern professional juggler. Highly skilled, he was feted in London by such writers as Thackeray and Hazlitt for his juggling and sword-swallowing acts, but (like Giovanni Piccini, the first known Punch & Judy man) Ramo Samee died in poverty. He can be seen on Frank's stage dressed in an embroidered cap and bow tie, holding the juggling balls. In his book Whanslaw notes how this trick is done. 'The balls are large, wooden beads and are threaded through hand strings, and special strings to the feet'.

Characteristically, Frank Edmonds chose to use trick dolls, figures which Whanslaw explains, 'require a little thought and experiment before they are perfect in action'. Edmonds's marionettes were seen by Percy Press in 1968, and he remarked that they were 'puppets suitable for showing in Drawing Rooms 15 to 18 inches but they were certainly very professional'. Edmonds was never afraid of showing off his considerable skills, which in the case of marionettes he had probably been obliged to re-learn. Punch, though, remained 'in his blood'. Throughout his life he had performed the show: he would surely never have consulted a book on the Punch & Judy show.

Edmonds may not have fully realised it, but in reviving marionettes he was part of a growing trend. In the later nineteenth century (when the Italian word *fantoccini* had been replaced by the French *marionette*) there had been a revival of travelling string puppet shows. Portable pavilions toured the country in family troupes, 'each touring its own rural circuit' – as George Speaight has described in his *History of the English Puppet Theatre* – performing dramas and pantomimes. The coming of the 'Kinema' diminished them, and the outbreak of the First World War finished them off.

Most of the men who had operated the theatres were conscripted and never returned to puppetry – if indeed they returned at all.

One well-known troupe did make what might be called a posthumous reappearance. Clunn Lewis was an Irish Catholic showman, who toured the south of England with Middleton's Marionettes. In the 1940s the puppets he had co-owned with the Tiller troupe were discovered by George Speaight in a Lincolnshire barn where they had been stored for thirty years. After restoring them with 'an excitement as intense as that of any archaeologist delving among the ruins of Babylon or Troy', Speaight presented the marionettes in the Festival Pleasure Gardens in 1951. 'Londoners could again drink beer and wine beneath the trees, and listen to the band, gaze at the fireworks down the fountain vista, and watch the puppets beside the flowing Thames'.

The major marionette revival of the early twentieth century was an artistic one. Among those involved was Walter Wilkinson's brother, with whom Walter had toured before he took up with his Peep Show. Arthur Stanley Wilkinson (1882–1957) began making marionettes in 1914 after watching a performance of Italian folk puppets. Increasingly concerned about the neglect of puppetry in England, in 1923 he founded the Marionette Society, giving an inaugural performance at the Poetry Bookshop, 35 Devonshire Street, London. His puppets included such Commedia dell'Arte figures as Harlequin and Pantaloon. Arthur Wilkinson went on to marry Lily Gair, and together they worked as the Gair Wilkinson Marionettes.

The Poetry Bookshop published a famous series of chapbooks, to which one contributor was Edward Gordon Craig, whose 'Puppets and Poets' appeared in 1921. The son of actress Ellen Terry, Craig (1872–1966) began his career as a player in actor-manager Henry Irving's company. He became a stage designer, creating stark sets in startling colours, gorgeous purples or muted greys, and experimenting with light.

In 1908 Craig published the first number of his magazine *The Mask*. The second number included his essay 'The Actor and the Über-Marionette' (or super-marionette). Written in Florence, it argued that marionettes are superior to living actors because they are unaffected by the audience's response, they are 'men without egotism'. Since Craig had been an actor himself, he knew just how they could behave, how emotion could mar a performance, coming between play and public. 'The actor must go, and in his place comes the inanimate figure – the *über-marionette* we may call him, until he has won for himself a better name.' Understandably, this caused an outcry, since it seemed to suggest that puppets should be substituted for living actors. Later, Craig attempted to explain his position, claiming that he did not wish to see living actors 'replaced by things of wood…The über-marionette is the actor plus fire, minus egotism; the fire of the gods and demons, without the smoke and steam of mortality'.

In the same year, a crucial one in his life, he was invited by Constantin Stanislavski to produce *Hamlet* at his Moscow Art Theatre. Craig, who had a remarkable ability to work equally well on either a small or large scale, created a model theatre to explain the play to the actors, using flat white figures carved in thin wood. The figures were afterwards inked and impressed on paper, thereby becoming Black Figures, 'half-woodcut, half-marionette' (which were used to illustrate the Cranach Press edition of the play).

Craig kept collections of marionettes, and for a year brought out a monthly magazine on the subject. Like Arthur Wilkinson, he thought that

62. Young Gobbo and Old Gobbo by Edward Gordon Craig, 1909

string puppets were being neglected, or regarded as suitable only for children. He valued marionettes much more highly, and exploited their possibilities to the utmost. He became the president of the British Puppet and Model Theatre Guild (a branch of the International Union of Marionettes) which was founded in 1925 by H. W. Whanslaw and Gerald Morice after the publication of Whanslaw's *Everybody's Theatre* two years earlier. Frank Edmonds was a member of the Guild.

Marionettes were now being discussed and used in performance; they became the subjects of some radical experiments. When Frank Edmonds first learnt about them as a child it was at a period when they were slipping out of favour. By the time he considered using them again, they were back on the centre stage. The figures he selected were ones which were difficult to manipulate, yet also traditional, harking back perhaps to his childhood memories of marionette performances.

By a happy coincidence Mark Poulton, Weymouth's current Punch & Judy man, has chosen to use those same figures in his own marionette show. He too will have a booth which can be used for both glove puppets and marionettes, which he believes will now be the only one of its kind, and unique to Weymouth.

Not all Punch & Judy showmen would be able to operate both of these very different types of puppet. Frank Edmonds could do it, from among his many outstanding manual skills. As a member of the Conservative club in Chester as well as in Weymouth, he played snooker and billiards for both towns' teams. He was a champion player, and had a cabinet full of trophies. In Chester he once played an exhibition match against world champion Joe Davis and won the game. 'He also played cards at both clubs', his grandson Frank has said. 'And I doubt if he lost often either'.

The Conservative club in Weymouth was at 5 King Street near the railway station and a stone's throw from the beach. It would also have been useful for a drink or two after the long hours of performance, which must have created quite a thirst.

Frank was a well-liked figure in Weymouth – the face behind Mr. Punch. His grandson says that 'he was very much at ease in company, and

63. The winning team. Frank Edmonds top row, second left

in front of a camera. He was an excellent speaker, he would have been able to make a living from after-dinner speaking these days, I would think'. He had a dry and cutting wit which would have come across well, though it was not always appreciated by his audiences. Punchman John Styles, commenting on one of Edmonds's evening Punch & Judy shows, remarked on how 'there were lots of little lines, throwaways. The audience laughed at the more obvious things. There were things he did that they didn't laugh at but which I found amusing. I felt somehow we were on the same wavelength'.

An interview recorded in 1967 provides a rare opportunity to hear Edmonds speak. He had a low, pleasant voice with his Chester accent sounding through, and he talked readily and easily about his working life. At the age of sixty-four, he was continuing to do seven shows a day in the high season, which he said affected his voice by the evening. He did not get tired, he continued, but used any opportunity in the performance to rest either arm 'a little' when it was not holding a puppet.

In this interview, for perhaps the first time, he mentioned the play's violence and the possible effect of this on the children in the audience, There were still a large number of adults (the 'young at heart') watching the show. In 1959 Edmonds was claiming that there were four adults to every child watching his show, and he does not seem to have made many changes to make his performance more child-centred, although in 1953 he included a road safety routine in his act. And by 1962, the hanging scene was becoming a rarity.

While Edmonds was no longer using the hanging scene regularly, he may have included it in the special late evening shows, along with cracks about politics and other topical affairs. His Boxers had always kept up with the times. Among the sparring pairs were Sugar Ray Robinson & Randolph Turpin, Floyd Patterson & Ingemar Johansson, Henry Cooper & Cassius Clay. No boxer ever emerged as a winner, going three inconclusive rounds in the little ring. Dawn Gould recalled that 'as they got "tired" they would do a most fantastic slow-motion fight, which was wonderful to see'. Punchman Martin Bridle, brought up in Weymouth, also described the act.

> He had a big preamble to the boxing match with a punch bag that came down from the roof. It was more like a ball held top and bottom by elasticated rope. There was quite a bit of byplay with Joey and Punch hitting the ball then Joey dodging away and it hitting Punch's nose. Then they spent quite a long time putting up the ring with a mallet, and Punch putting his nose at the end of the upright and Joey about to hit it and then not. Then he'd have these little boxers. They had big leather gloves that made a slapping noise. I think I remember his boxers making nondescript funny noises. "Hoi, ho, hump, ha, ho, cha!" Then in between the rounds they'd flop over the front, bodies panting up and down and heavy breathing into the microphone. Then they'd jump up again and knock each other around until the third round when they slowed down and knocked each other out.

Much use was made of the slapsticks down each side of the proscenium, each held loosely by a pin at the top, which can be seen in photographs of the postwar booth. When a doll's head was knocked against either of them, it made a 'resounding crack'. Incongruously, the contest-

64. Views of the booth. Slapstick top right and bottom left

ants were clad in coordinating woolly jumpers (knitted by Edmonds?) and long, flopping trousers.

The matches on which these fights were modelled had originated in the fair booths, where they provided one of the sideshows. The fighting was at first bare-knuckled, until the Marquis of Queensbury rules were introduced. Like Frank's puppets, boxers in the fairs fought in simple roped-off rings.

The Chinese Plate-Spinners too were used by Edmonds in longer shows, including the evening performances which drew enormous crowds. Vic Banks remembers the Chinamen as having pointed heads with metal spikes on which the 'rather heavy' plates were balanced. The juggling went on for about eight minutes, with no opportunity to rest either arm. Dawn Gould described how 'the plates would spin for ages and would be thrown from one performer to another, and I never saw one drop ever'. Martin Bridle remembered the Plate-Spinners too.

> With the Chinese jugglers a character came up spinning a plate on a stick. He tossed it up and down a few times. Then another came up with a stick and the first threw the plate over. This whole routine was very popular with the adults because it was a display of skill…I remember in the finale the second character spinning another plate and they went to toss each to the other. I can certainly remember him missing this move and the whole crowd gasping. It could have been a deliberate miss. That's a typical showbiz thing. Then they got the plates spinning again and succeeded and got a great reaction. It looked big. The two little puppets spinning those plates high in the air was good, very good.

65. From the left: Dr. Jeremy Cratchett, Basham,, Joey the Clown, Mr. Crow, Chinese Juggler, Biffam and Knockabout

This virtuoso performance must have been doubly satisfying to Edmonds: he was displaying the sort of skills which might have been used by his grandfather.

Punchmen in the mid-nineteenth century left the streets to perform in the drawing-rooms of the well-to-do, where little attention would be paid to the effect that the violence of the show might have on the children. After all, they were regularly beaten, infant mortality was high – and, not so long before, children had been taken to witness public hangings to teach them a moral lesson. Morality was to the fore here: the Devil, for instance (usually in the shape of a Bogeyman) would carry wicked Punch away. Mr. Punch's defiance of society's rules was muted in these shows, but the gusto with which he wielded his stick was less remarked. Not until after the Second World War were any serious concerns expressed about the violence. In his 1967 interview Edmonds remarked cheerfully that his show could be 'horrific'. The children loved it, he said, and came back for more. It was all in the way the material was put over: his show was funny. It was not a charge he took particularly seriously because he never had any complaints.

Edmonds had other more important matters to occupy him. In a previous interview of 1959 he told a reporter from the *Weymouth Echo* that 'I used to be able to make enough money here to keep me throughout the winter. Now money is tighter and I have a hardware business in Chester to see me through the year'. As well as appearing with Punch at parties and functions during the winter, Edmonds worked as a hardware dealer, a middleman, selling to other traders and shops or in the markets. He'd buy enamelware in the Midlands – mainly Wolverhampton and Bilston – and sell it on. His son Nick used to accompany him

66. Grandson Frank bottling

from the mid 1950s to the early sixties and says that 'Standing at a stall on a freezing day in Warrington is no fun, believe me!' Edmonds's main financial problem in Weymouth was that visitors (who formed the greater part of the audience) assumed that the performances of 'Weymouth's Own Show' were subsidised by the Corporation, and that the collections were merely an extra perk. (This assumption continues to be a problem for Punch & Judy showmen, including Weymouth's.)

Almost imperceptibly, the English seaside holiday was sliding into decline – an extended, slow and uneven process. With their rapid recovery after the War most resorts, including Weymouth, experienced a surge in visitors – especially as increasing numbers of workers were receiving longer holidays with pay. So, although more people were taking holidays abroad now that they had the opportunity (1.5 million in 1951, and up to five million in the 1960s), other people had a greater opportunity to travel, and this for a while masked any decline. However, as John K. Walton has pointed out, 'the British holiday scene was depending more on an older and increasingly working-class market with limited staying and spending power, and on shorter second holidays or long weekends for the more affluent, flexible and mobile groups'. While the former would have expected to see a Punch & Judy show on the beach, the latter might not be so interested.

Weymouth is on the edge of the south-west, an area which survived the decline better than most, perhaps due to the additional rural charms which lay beyond the boundaries of the resorts, now that visitors were inclined – thanks to the increasing use of cars – to travel around, rather than stay in one place. Most of the English seaside resorts inevitably suffered when cheap flights to hotter foreign beaches became widely available. With the experience which came from its history as one of the earliest watering places, Weymouth took measures (not always wisely) to halt the decline, which was to leave some resorts in a state of shabby stagnation and depression from which they have never recovered. As he retired in 1976, Frank Edmonds escaped the worst of the doldrums, just as he managed to miss the bugbear of political correctness which blighted the Punch & Judy show in the 1980s.

Lyme Bay

Weymouth's railway station had opened in 1857, and Swanage station in 1885. Lyme Regis's station, however, did not open until 1903, when a branch line was extended from Axminster. By 1908 it was possible to get from Waterloo to Lyme Regis in under three and a half hours, and the arrival of this light railway soon changed the nature of the resort. Old Lyme had attracted long-staying visitors, who came to hunt for fossils, to take the waters and to admire the town's spectacular setting. Or, as *Dunster's Guide* put it in 1896, Lyme 'possesses fascination for the poet, the artist, the botanist, the geologist, the lover of the picturesque, and the seeker after health'. With the railway came the day-trippers, in pursuit of pleasure, followed by a rag-tag of hawkers, buskers and Jacks-of-all-trades who hoped to make a profit by supplying their needs. With them too came the Punch & Judy show. There's a photograph from around 1913 of an anonymous booth on the Lower Walk (or Cart-road) above the beach, surrounded by a crowd of onlookers. This was probably the first show to

67. Punch & Judy show in Lyme Regis, circa 1913

appear in Lyme. Other shows seem to have followed in a fragmentary and piecemeal fashion. It was hard to make a living in the little resort.

The Revd. Glanville Magor performed at the Cobb end of the beach in Lyme Regis during the early 1990s, though his show had much older roots. He used a whole host of characters from Punch, Judy, Baby, Toby, Doctor, Constable, Beadle, Jack Ketch the Hangman and the Crocodile to Judy's Ghost (with spooky wire fingers), the Devil and the Black Man (in Nigerian dress as Glanville Magor had spent three years in that country). There were some more historic figures too – the Blind Beggar, Pretty Polly, a guitar-playing Scaramouch, the Courtier with his serpentine neck, and Hector the Hobby Horse. Revd. Magor even had his personal Parson, a cleric with a tube concealed in his mouth who sprayed the audience as he spoke. There were further characters that Magor made his own – the Lord Chief Justice, the Magician and the Mayor.

For a short while he also had a Councillor. While he was in Lyme, the Town Council had debated the by then rather tired topics of violence and sexism in Punch & Judy. There was a single objector to the show, who lost the vote by 23–1. By way of reply, Glanville Magor made a Councillor puppet, who met the usual fate at Punch's hands – after which the body was minced in the sausage machine. The sausages rolled out in the same colours as the dissenting Councillor's clothes, with a pair of pink bloomers to round things off.

But Glanville Magor didn't stop there. He made a politically correct Punch, complete

68. Glanville Magor in the pulpit with his politically correct Punch

with Marigold gloves, apron and a duster. As one of three clerical Punch & Judy men attending the May Fayre in the churchyard of St. Paul's, Covent Garden, every third year he would give a sermon in the church, to which, traditionally, Punch added a few words. The church was packed with Punch & Judy men, and stilt-walkers leaned against the pulpit. Magor spoke with Mr. Punch on his right hand and the domesticated Punch on his left.

69. 'Two Punches'

Some of his puppets were made of jelutong, a Malaysian timber not unlike balsa wood, which is used by pattern makers. It is soft and therefore easy to carve, but bruises easily, so Magor used the more traditional and tougher English lime for characters which took a battering. He made all his own costumes too.

Glanville Magor also carved marionettes (consulting H. W. Whanslaw's book on the subject). He used Commedia dell'Arte string figures in demonstrations during his work as a senior lecturer in religious education. He made a marionette of himself holding a smaller marionette of himself, holding a tiny Punch puppet which was very tricky to operate.

He said that he had come late and accidentally to Punch & Judy in

Cornwall during the 1970s. He was given a set of well-carved figures in 'terrible' costumes. Some of the figures were 'continental' and would not fit easily into an English show. Interested, he began reading up about them, and making puppets for himself. He learnt how to swazzle Punch, even having a clip put in his dentures to hold the instrument, which was never satisfactory.

Becoming well-versed in the history of Punch & Judy, on which he lectured, Magor regarded the beach show, with some notable exceptions, as 'a poor thing' – both brief and unpolitical. The anti-establishment side of Punch had gone: the side that presented 'the common man's point of view', in opposition to the family, the law and organised religion. When Punch left the street in the mid-nineteenth century and went into the parlour, the play was bowdlerised and much was lost.

After leaving Lyme Regis, Glanville Magor worked for nine years at Ironbridge Gorge Museum in Blists Hill Victorian Town. He performed with a live Dog Toby, a black and white collie called Bonnie, who could pick out aces and do sums, barking twice for yes and three times for no. She could also recognise the numbers one to four when they were held up before her. Glanville had a secret way of communicating with his dog: in all of the nine years only two people noticed his method. Bonnie was useful, too, in drawing the crowds.

Joey the Clown introduced the show in his 'Italian English', summoning Punch to the stage. The Crocodile might put in an appearance at the beginning 'to get him out of the way'. Amongst the old traditional characters, he is a comparative newcomer, too late in the day for Magor's tastes. The real action begins when Judy discovers Punch kissing Pretty Polly in the parlour, and sets upon Punch, who responds in kind.

The backcloth is then raised to reveal a street scene through which the Doctor enters, mounted on his Hobby Horse. He gives medicine to the dead Judy, revealing in an aside to the audience that that the potion is a sham. Unluckily for the Doctor, Punch overhears him, and he becomes the second victim.

Punch is arrested by the Beadle. The gaol scene swings round from the side, and the Lord Chief Justice pronounces a sentence of death on our hero. (The case has gone to the highest court.) The Hangman tries – and fails – to execute Punch, hanging himself in the process.

The gaol folds back to the street scene. Judy's Ghost then appears, or sometimes the Parson, intoning 'let us spray', which he immediately proceeds to do. At last the Devil makes his entrance, only to be killed by Punch. Joey pops up again and calls Punch to take a triumphant bow at the end of a show which Piccini himself might have found familiar. [For Glanville Magor's summary of the history of Punch & Judy see Tailpiece Three.]

Professor Brian Davey's is a very different kind of show. He and his wife Alison worked the sandbar end of the beach in Lyme Regis from around 1995 to 2001. They had been approached by the manager of Lyme's Marine Theatre about performing in the forecourt there, or inside the building if it rained. They tried it during a weekend of glorious sunshine to very small audiences: everyone was down at the other end of the beach.

On the manager's advice, Brian then approached the Town Clerk for permission to perform on the sands. The Council was very obliging, and granted him a concession at a peppercorn rent, merely requesting that he found a suitable pitch and kept to it. They even threw in a parking permit. Their chosen site was ideal, alongside the bouncy castle, the bathers and the deckchairs.

Brian and Alison worked a six week season during the school summer holidays. Though financially never very rewarding, in

70. Brian & Alison Davey

71. The Daveys' show in Lyme

Lyme Regis

performance terms some days were 'grim' and others 'fabulous'. Many adults watched the show, often out of nostalgia for their own childhoods. A groundsheet was spread in front of the booth which attracted both children and loose change. Alison, too, was a brilliant bottler, which was fortunate as many members of the audience failed to grasp 'the concept of paying for something which appears to be free'. If they were not sitting on the mat, or were standing at the back, why should they proffer their fifty pence? Alison would sometimes stop the show and shame them into paying up.

The couple variously describe their show as 'family-orientated', 'avuncular' and 'deliciously violent'. As well as bottling, Alison acts as a clown, a sort of 'Merry Andrew', standing by the booth and addressing Punch or the audience – whose participation is much encouraged. The audience know what they want; they 'make the show work'.

In Lyme they did three different shows on the beach; their shows are funny, with puns and slapstick, they are full of characters and alive with movement. Brian has a striking and colourful cast of dolls, all of which he makes himself. He carves them from wood, and paints their features. He makes puppets for other showmen too, among which are spitting images of Tony Blair and George Bush.

Brian and Alison are both artists who met at art school. Brian worked as a graphic designer, then became self-employed, doing book illustration during the vicissitudes of the Thatcher years. The puppet business was at first a sideline, until he let it take him over. After five hard years the couple began to earn a living (though never a large one) from Punch & Judy.

Brian researched scripts of the play and tried them out on his audiences. Generally he found that more authentic scripts would work while 'flowery elaborate ones' failed to hold attention. He stresses the visual aspects of the show, which works well in Europe as a result, minimising the language barrier. He has borrowed elements from the performances of two other artist showmen, Martin Bridle and Rod Burnett.

Brian and Alison have used two live Dog Tobies: a collie who died in 1998 and Midge, a Jack Russell cross which looked the part but proved 'useless' as it disliked the audiences. Now they use a doll for Toby.

Judy is played as a pantomime dame, who gives as good as she gets, bashing Punch with the stick. The Policeman comes from the school of Plod ('allo, 'allo, 'allo) while the Crocodile, with his big, crossed eyes, is much milder than most of his kind. Joey, latterly a Grimaldi figure, warns the children about Punch at the beginning of the show and tells him off at the end. While Joey survives, the rest of the cast are 'done away with': they are puppets, they will return another time.

In the past, Brian and Alison included the hanging routine and had no problem with it, saying (as Edmonds did) 'it's not what you do, but how you do it'. However, they found that children didn't understand the purpose of the gallows. As for Jack Ketch the Hangman – a masked figure in striped socks – he was usually mistaken for either Batman or a robber. It's a pity in a way that the Hangman lost his job in the show as he had some good jokes ('you'll have to get the hang of it' he tells Punch). Brian still uses the sausage machine, but in an updated style. Punch rocks the Baby and lowers it into the machine, and the Baby emerges as sausages… but wait. This is a recycling machine – turn the handle the other way, and the Baby reappears intact.

Brian uses the Devil too, a hairy-legged doll with cleft feet and a horned and fiery head who, despite his best efforts, fails to make off with Punch. This play goes through the whole gamut of emotions, from love to hate, from fear to laughter. Brian and Alison continue to perform it regularly – though, sadly, no longer in Lyme.

West Bay, between Lyme and Weymouth, has only ever known one Punch & Judy man, John Rodber, who performed there for about twenty-five years.

Before the Second World War, John Rodber worked for the Westminster Bank. He had been to art school and performed puppet shows in his spare time. As the Bank did not allow employees to make money elsewhere, all his shows were for charity. Called up, Rodber also did puppet shows in the Army when he was sent to Canada. Later, he was stationed in Naples, where he contracted polio. Though he was 'fragile' for a while, he was comparatively lucky; the disease caused only low level muscle damage to his leg.

John Rodber had met his wife Joy while she was an evacuee in Somerset, and in 1948 the couple bought a house with an adjoining building in Bridport. The property was on sale for £2,750. It was in a dilapidated state with a jungle of a garden, and needed a new roof. They offered £1,750 for it, money saved by Joy Rodber from her wartime

72. John Rodber carving Dog Toby

73. Dog Toby in action, with Punch

Army payments, and the offer was accepted.

John hated returning to work at the Bank, which was now in Crewkerne, and Joy urged him to leave. His employers were incredulous – such an early departure was unheard of – and wanted to send him to a psychiatrist. He left instead.

So now the Rodbers had a house, and John's small disability pension, which covered only rates and taxes. Soon they also had a family of four daughters. To earn a living, they opened the adjoining premises as an art shop, which served Bridport for many years.

Then, in about 1950, Rodber began performing Punch & and Judy, a show which gave the family a much-needed extra income. He carved his faces, hands and feet out of pinewood, and his wife dressed the figures. Early on (until he moved into the hall by the campsite) he gave shows at Gapes Yard, which was below the Wesleyan Chapel in West Bay.

Until 1884 and the coming of the railway, West Bay was known as Bridport Harbour, and was a small commercial port. Even in the 1950s there was not much for holiday-makers to do. The Rodbers gave shows after tea on every fine day, at around 5–6pm when their shop was closed. Queues would form even in the rain, in the hope that the weather might improve.

Gape Yard was where the horses which drew the pebbles off the beach were kept. Punch horses looked over their stables doors at Mr. Punch performing in his booth. Lobster pots were clustered in the roof. Muscovy ducks had to be shooed away by Joy, whose other tasks included collecting the money – sixpence for children and a shilling for adults – and evicting little boys from out of the booth 'by their britches'.

74. St. George (with salmon tin hat) defeating Hitler

The audience sat on the lifeboat, which was stored there, or on benches.

In later years, the Rodbers did television work as well. On one occasion Westward Television commissioned a performance in Weymouth, and sent a long white Rolls Royce car with a horn on the front to collect them. (They also paid well.) Joy made papier-mâché dolls which were used in these shows – an evil fairy, a sequinned snake, a jumping frog and a large pink pig.

Rodber used rod puppets and did conjuring too – his wife says he was 'terrible at it', though he didn't seem to care.

At Christmas, John performed at parties three or four times a week, leaving Joy to mind the shop and look after their small children. He continued to perform in West Bay until about 1975; he died in 1977.

The puppets are carefully housed in 'Great Aunt Audrey's sea chest' in the family's drawing room. There's a full set of Punch & Judy figures – Rodber used a traditional script – including a magnificent Toby, a moonish baby and a green-faced Devil. They are strong and individual. Joy's papier-mâché figures are witty and vivid. Although there are puppets galore, there are unfortunately no photographs of the performances in West Bay: John and Joy Rodber were too busy to take them.

Trade Secrets

I still work in the old style.

Frank Edmonds

Frank Edmonds's chosen trade had secrets of its own, which were carefully protected and preserved by Punch & Judy men.

Most secret was the lingo – the *parlaree* – which Frank could speak, to the bewilderment of some members of his family. The word parlaree, like most of its vocabulary, comes directly from Italian, in this instance from *parlare*, to talk. The Punch & Judy man interviewed in Henry Mayhew's mid-Victorian *London Labour and the London Poor* actually describes it as 'broken Italian'. Italian is the language of puppetry; and Italy is Mr. Punch's native land, where types of puppet are precisely defined, and may have different names in different regions of the country. There are several terms for a booth, too, and even a word for a bad puppeteer. In England, the Punchman famously seen by Samuel Pepys in 1662 was Pietro Gimonde of Bologna, and the first recorded script was based on a performance by another Italian, Giovanni Piccini. So Punch was an 'Italian immigrant' both as a marionette and as a puppet, and he brought some of his native language with him.

An Italian accent comes through now and again in John Payne Collier's transcription of Piccini's play – in the Prologue, for example, and again in a speech made by Punch to Scaramouch: 'I no like you playing so well as my own. Let me again. How you like that tune, my good friend? That sweet music or sour music, eh?' Piccini began his English career by performing in Italian, but later gave shows in his adopted tongue.

Anglicised Italian forms the basis of parlaree, interspersed with words from other lingua franca such as Yiddish and Romany – languages of those who may wish to keep things among themselves. 'Mozzy', for example, is from the Italian *moglie*, a wife, and can also mean Judy; 'scarper' is from *scappare*, to escape. 'Bonar' from the Italian *buono* meaning good. Romany words include *vater*, to watch, which also gives *vadring*, watching, and *chavvies*, which means children.

[For a glossary of parlaree words, see Tailpiece Two.]

Parlaree was also known to other showmen, to dealers and to travellers. It was most often used to discuss money matters, or to warn of potential dangers. The language was originally used by actors and showmen in the fairgrounds (actors, especially itinerant ones, were 'a despised class' until late in the nineteenth century) and Punch too would have been performing at the fairs. According to Henry Mayhew, parlaree was a mid-nineteenth century phenomenon. In 1851 he observed that 'the showmen have but lately introduced a number of Italian phrases into their cant language'. There were hierarchies of cant; Mayhew's Punch & Judy man claimed that parlaree was 'much higher than costers' lingo', which consisted mainly of backslang, and Mayhew seemed of the same opinion. He remarked that 'the slang language of the costermongers is not very remarkable for originality of construction; it possesses no humour: but they boast it is known only to themselves … The *root* of the costermonger tongue, so to speak, is to give the words spelt backward, or rather pronounced rudely backward'. It is still in use. Circus people use backslang too, mixed with Cockney rhyming slang and a sprinkling of Romany words. They often use parlaree words as well.

In an essay on the subject, Eric Partridge wrote that parlaree cannot really be called a language. It has no syntax or grammatical rules and a disregard for masculine/feminine

75. The London Costermonger

distinctions. Parlaree 'is a glossary, a vocabulary, not a complete language. Little remains. Even that little may disappear.' Decimalisation was to make quite a few words redundant. Yet at the point when it was beginning to fade, the language found another use as a secret code – amongst gay people while homosexuality was still illegal. In the 1960s radio programme *Round the Horne* Julian and Sandy (played by Hugh Paddick and Kenneth Williams) were two flamboyantly camp out-of-work actors who spoke in 'Polari', with Kenneth Horne as their innocent comic foil. Frank Edmonds loved the programme, which he found hilarious. He used to laugh and laugh and laugh, just as he had at his father's Punch & Judy performances.

In parlaree a Punch & Judy man was known as a *swatchel omi*, a Punch man, a man defined by his voice. The swatchel or swazzle, used by all Punch & Judy men worth their salt, is a further trade secret. The instrument consists of two curved metal plates enclosing a strip of tape, tied together with thread and inserted into the back of the mouth. It's individually shaped to sit properly in the throat. The tape is moistened by spit and blown through, just as children blow through grass blades stretched between their fingers. The swazzle is used rather than the voice box to produce Punch's infamous squawk – the sound which gave him his Italian name, Pulcinella, from *pulcino* or 'little chicken'. In Italy, the sound was produced by a *pivetta*, in France by a *sifflet-practique* and by a *pishchik* in Russia. (Mr. Punch is a well-travelled chap.)

Mayhew's showman claimed that Giovanni Piccini brought 'the calls, or unknown tongues' into England 'and we who are now in the purfession have all learnt to make and use them'. He said that he learnt the craft from Piccini himself, and that there were several types of swazzle: for indoor and outdoor use, for 'speaking and singing' and for selling. Like learning the violin, mastering the call was best done in 'out-of-the-way places', where no one else could hear you. Once the skill had been perfected, 'we can pronounce each word as plain as a parson, and with as much affluency'.

Anyone interested in learning how to use a swazzle should follow Glyn Edwards's full and lucid instructions in his *Successful Punch & Judy*, though even given such detail, there's still a great gap between theory and practice, and it's not just Tony Hancock who has been afraid of swallowing the swazzle! It's said, too, that you are not a true Punch & Judy professor until you've swallowed the instrument three times.

Punchman Stan Quigley told some tales about the swazzle. He liked to assure people that, should they swallow one, 'they would talk like Punch for the rest of their lives.' He also claimed that in the days when pieces of pewter tankards were still used, the swazzles would not work 'till they had been moistened with beer.' In 1895, another Punch & Judy man, Professor Jesson, went so far as to claim that anyone who swallowed the swazzle would afterwards die.

Frank Edmonds was an expert at 'the calls' and as a young man would play practical jokes on people with them. In the old way he swazzled Judy as well as Punch – theirs was a marriage made in a chicken coop. He also swazzled his Bogeyman, who emitted what has been described as a 'sort of buzz' or 'a strange whirring sound'. He often sang music hall songs in the warm-up to his act: singing through the swazzle produces far less strain on the voice.

Frank made his swazzles from silver bangles which he cut to shape and into which he inserted pre-boiled herring-bone tape. He used one swazzle during each show, though he always had a spare, in case he did swallow one. When he was showing at parties and the like, using his portable show, he always kept his swazzles in an old snuff box, as his grandson Frank remembers.

Like his brothers, Frank Edmonds learnt the Punch & Judy play as a boy from watching his father's show. In the past, many showmen came from Punch & Judy families and learnt the play by watching their fathers, uncles or grandfathers perform. They were family plays. Only more recently have performances been based on published versions of the show; even then they are generally combined with material gathered from watching other performers.

The old way, Frank believed, was the right way. In an interview with the *Dorset Evening Echo* in 1959, he said 'I don't mind admitting that the script I use is exactly the same as the one used by my father over 60 years ago.' As Harry Edmonds had described himself as a Punch & Judy man in 1901, this would make the script a very old one. And if – as Frank also seemed to believe – his grandfather Andreas had been a Punch & Judy man too, then his would be one of the earliest surviving scripts. In 1871, Andreas was described as a clerk, and Frank's maternal grandfather was known to have been a shoemaker. So either Harry was brought up by another relative, who may have been a showman – as previously suggested – or Andreas spent part of his life doing other, more financially rewarding and securer work. Certainly, the Edmonds play includes many characters and routines which were found in the Victorian period – the Beadle, the Crocodile and the voice of the Master; the Chinese Plate-Spinners and the Boxers.

The script published at the end of this book [as Tailpiece One] is a version remembered from the 1960s, which had obviously been adapted to suit the times, becoming (whatever Edmonds claimed to the contrary) inevitably more child-centred. Much remains, though, from older traditions. Frank was proud to be using the family play, and did not care if other Punchmen watched, or even recorded the performance. 'I don't mind,' he said, 'you please yourself. I lead, follow who can!'

The first published Punch & Judy script, that of the performance of Giovanni Piccini, appeared in 1828, not long before his death – thus both ensuring Piccini's immortality and providing an important document in the history of puppetry. The script was given the rather grand title of *The Tragical Comedy, or Comical Tragedy, of Punch and Judy*, and was illustrated by that superb artist, George Cruikshank. The anonymous author proved to be the writer and critic John Payne Collier, whose other main claim to fame was the publication of a partially forged Second Folio of Shakespeare's works. Unsurprisingly then, the script has a distinctly literary feel and comes with learned trappings: it has an introduction, a history of the show, a preface, a Prologue, and some detailed footnotes about the origins of the play. It's also hardly surprising that the text has been regarded with suspicion, thanks to Collier's dubious reputation and his vague and unsubstantiated claims to have added episodes from other sources. Yet Cruikshank observed that Collier noted down all Piccini's words at a special private performance, and they clearly correspond to the artist's cartoons which were sketched at the scene.

Piccini's play has some characters who are now seldom used, such as Punch's silent paramour, Pretty Polly (heroine of John Gay's 'extravagantly popular' *Beggar's Opera* of 1728), and an equally silent Courtier, who can stretch his neck like a goose and – in an exhibition of the puppeteer's expertise – doff his hat.

Most of the characters are more familiar. There's Punch, of course, and Judy, Baby, Dog Toby, the Doctor, the Police Officer, Jack Ketch the Hangman (who also features in the *Beggar's Opera*) and the Devil. There's Scaramouch who, like Punch, was a Neapolitan Commedia dell'Arte character. Piccini brought his own puppets with him from Italy, and thought the English ones inferior. He, and other Italian puppeteers who left their country at this troubled time in its history, probably based their performances on an Italian version of the play, which, according to John Payne Collier, was adapted by Piccini to be 'more to the taste of English audiences', though his backcloth remained resolutely and statuesquely Italian: half-timbered houses were a later development. Some of the show's characters were given English counterparts, like Pretty Polly and Jack Ketch the Hangman – Polly is found in eighteenth-century Italian glove puppet plays in the guise of a Young Woman. The Doctor is a lawyer in the Italian plays: here his services are needed more urgently as a medical man. One or two characters, like Hector the Hobby Horse, were of native origin. Punch himself emerges as a more dominant figure than he was as a marionette, occupying the puppeteer's right hand throughout most of the play. Unmasked and liveried, he looks different from his Italian counterpart Pulcinella, but behaves in much the same manner.

It's been argued that Piccini's script is meant to be read rather than performed (or, alternatively that it's better when performed) but either way it has the classic shape of the modern play, with Punch defeating a series of figures, representing various different types of authority, and its influence is undeniable: Piccini's journey across Europe was to have resounding consequences. Consciously or not, fragments of the dialogue, too, have been repeated down the years. Some of them can be found in the Edmonds family's version of the play.

The next printed version, *The Dominion of Fancy, or, Punch's Opera*, was included in Henry Mayhew's interview with a Punch & Judy man in his *London Labour and the London Poor*. Mayhew's unnamed showman had bought most of his puppets from Piccini (or 'Porsini' as he called him), but he used them to make a different, Cockney show, one which it is possible to visualise in performance. The showman, in his running commentary on the action, rather defensively insisted that his was a moral tale. He concluded that 'All this wit must have been born in me, or nearly so; but I got a good lot of it from Porsini and Pike [Piccini's apprentice] – and gleanings, you know'.

The third printed script, and the first intended for children, *The Wonderful Drama of Punch & Judy and their Little Dog Toby*, followed shortly afterwards in 1854. Its author, Papernose Woodensconce (journalist and playwright Robert Brough) wrote in his preface: 'The want of a good acting edition of *Punch and Judy* has long been felt, chiefly by ambitious young gentlemen aspiring to give private representations of that world-famous drama'. The show, with comic drawings by 'The Owl', moves at a cracking pace and is full of puns and jokes, but is cheerfully unfrightening, tailored to its primary audience. In Brough's version, for example, the Devil has

76. The Gho-o-o-o-ost!!!

become a 'Horrid, Dreadful Personage', who is easily diverted into carrying off the Hangman rather than seizing Punch. There is a Ghost (a Gho-o-o-o-o-ost!!!) who can only say 'Boo-o-o-oh!'

The very fact that plays for children were being produced – more were to follow – reveals how much the show was changing. Some of the Punchmen were by now performing in the genteel drawingrooms of the better-off, sometimes solely for the benefit of children. This inevitably affected the kind of play which was enacted. There's a new self-consciousness about this script.

But Punch & Judy is nothing if not versatile, and two other published scripts are of street shows. The 'book of the words' of Professor Mowbray of Notting Hill was published in *Pall Mall Gazette* on June 15 1887, probably the first time a Punch & Judy play appeared in a newspaper. According to Mowbray a script was even then a rare item, he said that there were only about 'fifteen of us left', a recurring refrain in the records of Punchmen. It's a short play, as street shows usually were (The performance of Mayhew's showman is notably protracted, perhaps because of the presence of the reporter.) An Alligator is among those listed in Mowbray's cast who does not appear, suggesting that a longer performance might be

given on occasion, or else the extent to which he varied the show. Like Brough's, the play has a live Toby. The pompous Beadle (a very Victorian official) survives four bashings, only to be hanged by Punch on his next appearance. Joey the Clown comes in to see the Beadle dangling from the gallows.

PUNCH: Here, mind out!
[*They pick up the Beadle*]

77. *Professor Mowbray by Professor Mowbray*

CLOWN: Put him in.
PUNCH: Put him in the coffin.
CLOWN: Put over the pall.
PUNCH: Put over St. Paul's.
[*They lift him up, execute a pas de deux in the midst of which the Ghost appears. Punch knocks him down.*]
PUNCH: Good bye. It's all over now! [*Exit*]

The show is brisk, full of puns, business-like and ticklish to perform, with much twirling of the bodies on Punch's stick. Another authentic-sounding script, that of Professor Smith 'of London' (probably of Selby Street, Poplar) was published by Hamley's in 1906 as *The Book of Punch & Judy*. This show lasted for three quarters of an hour. On one occasion the King and Queen stood and watched 'the *entire* performance, and were graciously pleased, to express their pleasure and amusement thereat.' As with Brough's version, the show featured a heated argument about the ownership of Toby. There's no Devil in Smith of London's play, his role is taken by the Crocodile. The show is rounded off with an energetic funeral scene for the hanged Hangman and the final appearance of Judy's Ghost:

PUNCH: (*screams*) Joey! Joey! Come up here. I've seen a ghost.
CLOWN: Seen a ghost! Get out! That's your imagination.
PUNCH: Well, you chain him up.
CLOWN: Chain who up?
PUNCH: Imagination.

In shows like these the play was changing, largely thanks to the mollifying influence of that jolly figure, Joey, but they were still not without some haunting variations on old jokes. Photographs of a further, fancier performance, that of Professor Jesson, were published in the *Strand* magazine in 1895. The accompanying script – referred to as the 'original' play – follows Piccini almost verbatim in the first act. Later deviations from the older show are carefully noted. Although Jesson was a member of a Punch & Judy dynasty, he seems to have learnt the play from Henry Bailey,

78. Professor Jesson's booth, 1895

'the best man that ever performed the dolls', and the notes make clear the gradual shift from Piccini's to Bailey's to Jesson's performance, providing a useful record of how the show developed. Unlike Bailey, for example, who 'made a great deal of this scene', Jesson does not use the Hobby Horse. Both men dispense with the Hangman and the Devil, the latter being 'the arch-enemy of mankind'. This ungodly duo are 'apt to harrow the feelings of the little ones and give them bad dreams'. Yet the extremely violent domestic scenes remained unaltered.

Probably dating from around the same period, the Edmonds family play seems closer in style to the Smith and Mowbray performances than to Jesson's, though like the latter's his opening scenes hark back to Piccini. Grandly, Frank Edmonds liked to claim that he never changed his father's script, but this was not so: his play naturally evolved over the sixty odd years of his performances. Piccini's play opens with Punch and Scaramouch arguing over the ownership of Toby (a stuffed animal in Piccini's version) and Frank used a version of this classic scene with 'Toby's Man', otherwise known as 'Mr. Jones,' who insisted he was the dog's proprietor. Mr. Punch's nose is invariably a casualty of the episode, one which Frank dropped when he stopped using a live animal in 1939. Both Scaramouch and Toby's Man lay into Punch, with Scaramouch wielding a stick which he calls his 'fiddel', the maker of 'sweet music'.

The scene with the Baby follows in both plays, although Edmonds appears to have cut or modified this in later years. Although the Baby meets its end more violently in Piccini's play, there's a moment of pure terror in the Edmonds version when Punch screams 'Judy, Judy the baby has no head,' only to discover he is holding the child upside down. Punch also squats on the Baby to restrain it, enabling him to make the old joke about 'baby-sitting'. Like the Baby's, Judy's death in Piccini's play is more terrible, particularly as at one chilling point she begs her husband for mercy. Both Punchmen twirl Judy's body, lifeless on Punch's stick.

Punch's murderous activities attract the attention of the law. Piccini's Officer utters the lines which can still be heard in the plays, including that of the Edmonds family.

79. Piccini's Scaramouch by George Cruikshank

OFFICER: We shall see about that. I've come to take you up.

PUNCH: And I've come to take you down

Representing the law, Frank Edmonds has both a Policeman and that pompous official, the Beadle, whose life in art was prolonged by his sinister appearance in Dickens's *Oliver Twist*. Dawn Gould remembered Frank's braided Beadle as having 'a deep sonorous voice' and being 'awfully scary'. He has another much-repeated exchange with Punch – first recorded by Mayhew, and used by Mowbray and Smith – as the two dolls fight it out.

BEADLE: That's a topper.

PUNCH: That's a whopper.

BEADLE: That's a good 'un.

PUNCH: That's a better 'un.

Both Mayhew's showman and Frank Edmonds continue with an interlude starring Joey, an English character modelled on Joseph Grimaldi, 'King of Clowns'. While there's a Clown in the succeeding plays, there's no Clown in Piccini's version (though in his preface Collier makes passing reference to Grimaldi's dancing). Piccini's play does however pay tacit tribute to the clown by including his catchphrase 'Don't be a fool now', made famous in Grimaldi's pantomime *Harlequin and Mother Goose; or, the Golden Egg*.

The fact that Merry Andrews are found in plays before 1828, suggests the Clown was featured before he was named for Grimaldi. But most of the clowns in Punch & Judy shows are called Joey, and have his decorated face and cockatoo hair. One well-loved scene – used by Edmonds, among many others – has Punch lining up the bodies of his victims on the playboard and attempting to count them. Punch is foiled in his efforts by the deft hand of Joey, who shuffles the corpses like a pack of cards. In the plays, as if in obscure tribute to his namesake's popularity, Joey invariably escapes the mass slaughter. Grimaldi was known to be fond of butterflies, and Frank sometimes had another scene in which Joey tried to catch one, both helped and hindered by Punch.

Other characters take on Punch in ascending levels of threat. In Piccini's play, Jack Ketch the Hangman puts in a grim appearance. Like his even madder contemporary, Hanging Judge Jeffreys, Ketch was a man of such brutality that he lived on long in folk memory. While Judge Jeffreys sentenced many of the men in the Monmouth Rebellion to death, Ketch hanged the Duke, their leader. In Punch's play, attitudes to execution were slow to change. There's an eighteenth-century feel to Piccini's hanging scene, which has a poignant familiarity with the fatal tree. When Ketch brings in the gibbet, Punch exclaims, 'Well, I declare now, that very pretty! That must be a gardener. What a handsome tree he has planted just opposite the window, for a prospect!' He affects to believe that the ladder is being brought 'to steal the fruit out of the tree' and that the coffin is 'a large basket for the fruit be put into'. Punch seems to be moving almost unwittingly towards his death until Jack Ketch summons him to be hanged.

PUNCH: You would not be so cruel.

J. KETCH: Why were you so cruel as to commit so many mur-
ders?

PUNCH: But that's no reason why you should be cruel, too,
and murder me.

But Punch of course outmanoeuvres Jack Ketch. This same Hangman
turns up in Mayhew's play, where he is also known as 'Mr. Graball', one
who 'takes all, when they gets in his clutches'. Another real-life hangman,
William Marwood, makes an appearance in other shows. Marwood (1818–
1883) was a devout Methodist and a 'shoe dealer' by trade. He was fifty-
four when he succeeded the incompetent William Calcraft as executioner.
His calling card read 'All Orders Promptly Executed'. None of Marwood's
executions was public, and due to the practical improvements he introduced, none of his victims was strangled or decapitated, as had often been
the case with his predecessor, of whom Marwood said, 'he hanged them,
I execute them'. Such improvements, however, did not change the fate of
his alter ego in the Punch & Judy show.

In Professor Smith's play, where he made an extended appearance, he
was billed as 'Master Marwood (the Executioner)' like some unlucky
Happy Families card. Gus Wood, one of the Punchmen rejected by Swanage Council, also featured Marwood in his performances. Frank Edmonds
had an unnamed Executioner, who ended the street shows of Edmonds
and his father, but who by 1962 was no longer appearing in every show.
A reporter on the *Weymouth Echo* thought that the omission was due to
pressure by worried parents. Yet he reported that whenever Edmonds
missed out the coffin and the hanging 'there are near tearful requests from
a horde of kids to put back that charade of innocent grue.'

Later on, Edmonds seems to have abandoned his executioner com-
pletely. He does not feature in the script included at the end of this book.
Public attitudes to hanging were changing, particularly after the execution
in 1955 of Ruth Ellis, the last woman to be hanged in England, sentenced
to death for the murder of her unfaithful lover, David Blakely. Her hanging caused an uproar, with angry demonstrations outside the prison. Ellis's

execution, and that of Derek Bentley in 1953 for a crime committed by his underage accomplice, left the system discredited, and in 1965 capital punishment was abolished by the Labour Government. Within a generation, the Hangman must have become a quaintly old-fashioned villain to young audiences.

The Devil, too, found himself being phased out. Like Bailey and Jesson, Mowbray and Smith do not have a Devil. Frank had a Devil in the 1930s; later he became a Bogeyman because, Edmonds said, 'you shouldn't call the Devil.' It offended people if you did. When swazzled, the inoffensive Bogeyman emitted a buzzing sound, more waspish than Satanic. Of greater importance to his play (and far more frightening) was the Crocodile, who held the stage with a prolonged appearance, demonstrating a good deal of confidence on the part of his puppeteer – the same confidence Edmonds demonstrated when he allowed others to borrow from his version of the play. Everyone who recalls his performance seems to remember these scenes best of all.

Professor Mowbray's is the first published script containing a scene with a Crocodile. Punch is sitting and singing a song when the Crocodile comes up and bites his hand. He knocks it away with his stick.

> Punch: Murder! Murder! Murder! What is it? I know what it is; it's a poor little pussy cat. No, it isn't; it's a Crocodile. [*He makes the Crocodile open its mouth and looks inside.*] I can see what he has had for his dinner. He has had sausages and pudding. I know it's a pussy cat. [*Punch sits by its side singing* "I love little pussy, her coat is so warm." *The Crocodile then gets hold of Punch's nose, and Punch pushes his stick down its throat. The Crocodile chases Punch round the show biting him in several places, and disappears. Punch then lies on the stage and calls for the Doctor.*]

In the Edmonds version, the Crocodile makes a leisurely entrance, appearing behind Punch, who of course does not notice his presence until he's actually been bitten. A voice from offstage – his Master's voice – informs Punch of what the audience already knows – 'It's a Crocodile!'

Punch tries to placate the beast by stroking its long green nose; the Crocodile responds by swallowing his stick. While retrieving the stick, Punch notices a string of sausages – one of Joey Grimaldi's favourite props – in the Croc's cavernous mouth. After a comic tussle, Punch manages to yank the bangers out. He makes an exultant exit – despite his bitten nose.

Next comes Mr. Crow, who enters singing and dancing and chatting casually with the audience. He sings 'Polly Wolly Doodle' and 'I Come from Mississippi'. Mr. Crow – Jim Crow, or a character like him – had appeared in Punch & Judy plays from the early days, treated with varying degrees of prejudice. Similar characters range from Piccini's 'Servant in a foreign livery' to Mayhew's showman's 'Jim Crow' to Mowbray's and Smith's 'Nigger'. Some of these figures are based on the American entertainer Thomas D. Rice's blacked-up character, itself said to be modelled on a crippled black stableman. Piccini's character, however, predates this.

In Frank's play, Mr. Crow is an amiable, laid-back sort of fellow, untroubled by his eventual discovery of the amphibian's presence. In fact, convinced the Crocodile won't harm him – he thinks everyone likes him – he nonchalantly slides down its nose. Then he gives the Crocodile his wooden leg to bite, as a dog might be given a bone to play with. He is still trusting the animal, and fails to realise what the audience knows will happen. In a moment

of real horror, the Crocodile gets a grip on Mr. Crow's good leg, and spins him, screaming, away for ever. Even more horrifying, perhaps, was Edmonds's 1950s variant on this scene, where Mr. Crow, after conducting his own singing, lets his hand drop slowly into the Crocodile's jaws, with predictably gruesome consequences.

80. Crocodile and Mr. Crow's leg

The Bogeyman causes considerably less bother to Punch, who soon dispatches him, having been warned of his presence by his Master. 'That's the first good thing you've done', says Joey, who arrives just in time to see this last body. Punch has triumphed. Though Piccini's show had an unmatched, elegant savagery; the Edmonds play is far pacier and much more funny.

Among the several nineteenth century elements in the Edmonds family play, the opening scene contained an echo of Piccini in Punch's address to the audience. 'You know, you know, say how you do. If you all happy, me all happy too', dating back to 1828. The Crocodile, though, came into the play in the mid-Victorian era – the earliest known photograph of a Crocodile puppet, in the show of Professor Smith of Ilfracombe, was taken around 1887. Harry Edmonds was born in 1871. If he learnt the play from his father Andreas, or from an adoptive showman parent, then the play could date back to the Crocodile's young days. It's undoubtedly an old script, into which Frank Edmonds introduced his own unmistakeable character.

While he liked to give the impression that the show remained the same, even in 1934 Edmonds told the *Southern Times* that although he still worked 'in the old style' in parts he put in 'some adapted scenes to make it more suitable for to-day.' Not only did Edmonds's show develop through the years, he also varied the performances – as outside performers are often obliged to do. The show would be shortened on rainy days, or during a sudden shower, or at times when the celebrated Weymouth sand blew grittily into the eyes of the watchers.

Longer shows on good days would involve more of his cast, including characters such as the Doctor, a quack who traded under several different names, like Dr. Cratchett or as Harry called him, Dr. Jollop. ('Jalop' is a Mexican plant used as a laxative, a Victorian joke which Frank decided to drop.) Other optional extras included the Ghost and the Policeman – and there were extra routines, too, like the spider, the punchball, the Chinese Plate-Spinners or the Boxers. In evening performances the more adult audiences would be given an extended show, containing some dry and knowing jokes about politics or current affairs. Such shows might well have been closer to the Victorian prototype of the Edmonds family script.

The End of the Show?

I never begrudged a second of it. I was always glad to have been a Punch & Judy man.

Frank Edmonds

S uddenly and unexpectedly, on June 1st 1964, Frank's longtime bottler, his brother Claude's son Sidney, died in Weymouth & District Hospital, aged thirty-eight. He had worked with his uncle since the War. In the summer they shared in a caravan, in the winter Sid worked as a lorry driver in Chester, where he lived in Beaconsfield Street.

After Sidney's death, his younger brother Joey came to Weymouth for

81. Joey and Frank Edmonds

the rest of the season. Frank Edmonds was already there, bottling for his grandfather and doing 'the chat with Mr. Punch'. He remembers Sid as 'a lovely man, and one for the ladies, I probably have lots of relations around

Weymouth thanks to him.' He also, of course, remembers Sid's death, which he thought was 'something to do with his stomach', possibly a perforated ulcer, attributed by his uncle to 'the large quantities of IPA he quaffed most evenings'.

> I remember the night Sid died, at the time the three of us were living in a caravan at the backwaters behind the fairground. I had been out on the town for the evening, when I returned to the caravan I found a note tied to the door handle, it was from the police asking us to contact the hospital. I wasn't sure where FE was, so I wandered about a few of his regular haunts, and found him playing cards at the Conservative club. We set off for the hospital straight away, walked in and were met by a doctor who said 'there's not much more you can do tonight, but you can take his personal effects with you.' We obviously looked shocked at this news, and the doctor then realised we hadn't known about Sid's demise, he thought the police had informed us, I don't think I've ever heard anyone be so apologetic in all my life. Sid's father Claude came down and arrangements were made to take Sid by train home to Chester.

Sid and Joey's father Claude Edmonds was a Punch & Judy man in Filey at that time. He had worked on various beaches in the north-east, including Sunderland and for 'over twenty years' at Whitby, but is probably best known as Filey's Punch & Judy man. A resort which is both dramatic and decorous, Filey has five miles of beaches, bordered to the north by The Brigg, 'a slippery green seaweedy causeway' as it was described in 1948, which reaches far out into the bay. The steep cliffs are incised by a ravine, and layered with tiers of stuccoed hotels and boarding houses.

Photographs from the guides of the 1960s show Claude's green-and-white-striped wooden booth in gardens just above the beach and the chilly North Sea. Like his brother's, his proscenium has a brightly coloured clown on either side, and displays the same Chester backcloth, with the unmistakable Rows and the Eastgate clock. Claude's show must have been similar too, as both men had learnt the play by watching their father perform.

Keith Ellis's mother was Prudence Edmonds, one of Claude's six chil-

82. Claude Edmonds in Filey

dren. He remembers family holidays in Filey in the 1960s, before Claude gave up his show and left to join his brother in Weymouth in 1968–69. He was allowed to watch from inside the booth, sitting on a box on the left-hand side. 'Watch while I bring these puppets to life', Claude would say. Later he offered Keith his puppets (which had been belonged to Harry Edmonds) but Keith 'adolescently' refused them, a decision he now regrets. The puppets were sold, though Keith Ellis still has his grandfather's swazzle, which he carefully preserves in a case.

No one in the family took over from Claude or from Frank, although Frank's elder son and namesake had helped him for a while. A radio interview of 1961 remarked that it was a shame that neither of his sons was 'entering the business'. The only person to show a sustained interest in performing was his grandson, the third Frank, who wrote:

> I think he was very disappointed, he was asked who if anyone was going to carry on the tradition during the television programme recorded in 1964, he thought his grandson might, but that no one else probably would. When he retired I asked him to sell me his

dolls, he went and sold them to someone else, without telling me. I am not sure whether it was because I had got a "proper job" and was unlikely to use them professionally, or not.

Sid Baldwins became Frank's regular bottler, and in 1966 the *Echo* reported on their working life together. 'It's a long day for the Punch & Judy men. Frank lives in a caravan and Sid lives at Wyke. They're down on the beach at 9.30 every morning through the season, which starts at Whitsun and stretches to the end of September, and they stay there till 8 o'clock at night.'

Then on September 14th 1966 the *Echo* reported that Frank Edmonds's youngest daughter Sylvia, a nurse, had been killed in a car crash along with her husband, Michael Krol. Their two small daughters, who were also passengers in the vehicle, were injured. Christine was thrown out of the car, while the other child, Angela, tried in vain to revive her mother, who had been thrown into the back of the car by the impact.

At the inquest in Chester Town Hall, Leonard Hutchings, a lorry driver, gave evidence that 'he was following the Krols' car along the main road through Thornton-le-Moors in the Wirral on August 25 when the driver, Mr. Krol, indicated he was going to turn right. A sports car was coming in the opposite direction. "Instead of stopping in the centre of the road, the driver then continued to negotiate the corner and collided with the sports car", he said. "The Krols' car spun round and ended up on its side." '

The news of their parents' deaths was broken to the two girls by a Catholic priest two weeks after the accident. Frank and his wife immediately decided that they would move to their daughter's home at 28 Greenbank Road, Chester 'so that the children could continue their former life as much as possible'. 'I don't know how this will affect my career', Frank was quoted as saying, 'but it is the least we can do for the kiddies'. Soon afterwards, though, the house was sold and the money put into a trust fund for the two girls. Angela and Christine moved into their grandparents' house in Western Avenue, Blacon, near Chester. Frank's eldest daughter Ivy brought up the children and they all lived together with Frances and her younger son Nick. So Frank was free to return to the

83. Three of Frank Edmonds's grandchildren outside the former family home, The Grange: Frank with Sylvia's daughters, Angela and Christine

beach in 1967.

It seemed as though there would be no Punch & Judy on Weymouth beach in the summer of 1969. On October 1st 1968 the *Dorset Evening Echo* announced that the show had been sold. It was bought by Weymouth antique dealer Leslie Poole of The Old Curiosity Shop, 23 Upper St. Alban Street, where sixteen of Edmonds's puppets were on display 'in a glass showcase in his showrooms'. Poole also bought a set of marionettes and two collapsible theatres 'none of which was ever used by Edmonds on the beach', the *Echo* claimed. He also acquired 'a walking stick with a silvered brass head depicting Punch' which had belonged to Andreas Edmonds, and a Victorian button hook. Poole said that he 'would like the future of the show to be connected with Weymouth in some way' and that he would not be selling the puppets separately.

Magicians attending a conference in Weymouth had already expressed interest in the purchase: 'The magicians who looked at the puppets in the Poole treasure house of antiquities were delighted with their find. When the name of Edmonds was mentioned there were nods of familiarity from most of them. Continental barriers, it seems, are no obstruction in the fame of the Edmonds puppet shows'. One of the magicians was Punchman Percy Press, who on October 4th reported on the sale in a letter to Gerald Morice.

84. Claude and Frank Edmonds

I saw the figures in their glass showcase and was told that they were considered to be about 200 years old, I promptly contradicted this pointing out that the dressing was fairly recent also the presence of a Policeman dated the outfit to me, after these remarks the young lady was more careful with her sales talk. I did not enquire the price but others did and I was told they wanted £250 for the complete outfit which included two fit-ups and a set of marionettes…

But Edmonds, like his chief puppet, popped up yet again, with his booth and dolls. As he'd said in more than one interview, he kept two sets of puppets, and he had probably sold his second-best ones, or so his grandson Frank has suggested. Michael Darrington, however, remembers booth and puppets changing after 1969, 'the booth became taller and more highly decorated and the puppets were a complete transformation, like upgrading from a Mini to a Rolls Royce!'

His grandson believes that 'he had genuinely decided to retire, he was after all 65 and was due his pension, the events of the previous couple of years had been difficult, losing his daughter and son-in-law, and having young children in the house again. Maybe he was just tired at the end of the season, but the winter lay off seems to have restored him. I don't think he really needed the money but he truly loved his work, and probably realised he would miss both the work and Weymouth; he had made lots of friends there.' So he was back the next season, assisted by Claude, with whom he shared a caravan, as Frank remembers. 'I used to go to Weymouth at least once a year during the summer, for my holidays, during the time Frank and Claude were there together, they shared a caravan which was sited at Seaview Caravan Park, 90 Camp Road in Wyke Regis, overlooking the Fleet lagoon. The site belonged at that time to a Mr. Jim Bennett; I would stay with them, and what a pair of cantankerous individuals they were. The TV programme Grumpy Old Men has nothing on them, they could moan for England, those two.' As its name suggests, Camp Road (formerly known as Green Lane) had been used by the Army. Frank bought a modern caravan, which featured electric lights and a fridge. There was still no bathroom, but the site had a toilet block and showers, so it was an improvement – and there was a club on the site. 'FE and Claude had their own seats in the corner by the bar; their names were even written on the wall above the seats.'

It was not until 1976 that Frank finally retired, at the age of 73. He put one set of puppets up for sale: the dolls and booth were bought by their present owner from an antique shop in Ringwood in 1978. In January

85. Frank Edmonds outside Guy Higgins's booth

1976 Edmonds told the *Echo* of his plans. He would come down from Chester around Easter as usual and stay in his Wyke caravan until the end of the summer. 'I love Weymouth – I always shall – but I'm getting a bit too old to go on working. I shall still carry out a few private engagements in the Chester area, but for me the long seaside season is over.' He added 'Now I'm going to relax by getting in the car and driving around the country looking for other Punch and Judy shows to watch'. When he returned to Weymouth, it would be as a holiday-maker. He definitely returned at least once, as a photograph shows him standing outside his successor Guy Higgins's booth, with what looks like an approving smile. Though of course in his heart he believed that there was only one Punch & Judy man better than himself – and that was his father, Harry.

In 1977, Frank Edmonds suffered a stroke, and he died of heart disease on July 26 1981 at the West Cheshire Hospital (now known as the Countess of Chester). His wife Frances predeceased him: she never really recovered from the loss of her daughter Sylvia. On October 3 1981, Gerald Morice reported the death of Frank Edmonds in the *World's Fair*, an event which seems initially to have been unnoticed by other Punch & Judy showmen. He wrote 'I have but recently heard of the death of the eminent Punch professor, Frank Edmonds, who passed away earlier this year. Mr. Edmonds worked the beach at Weymouth for 52 years, which must be something of a record, and he toured the British Isles before that. My information came from Professor Guy Higgins, who took over from him at Weymouth. Mr. Higgins only learnt the sad news the day before he wrote to me. A native of Chester, Frank Edmonds told Guy that he had actually walked and worked the various street pitches from Land's End to John o'Groats.'

In an interview done shortly before the end of Edmonds's life, Robert Leach asked him if he ever got bored performing the Punch & Judy show. He replied:

> 'I never got bored. The only man that got bored was Mr. Punch. Many a time he's looked down on me and said, "You're a silly old sod, you are, you know." ' To him, Punch seemed to be alive:

'Some days, he'd work like a human being. And other days he'd be just like me with a bad head. "What's the matter with you today Mr. Punch? Was you on the beer last night?" "No, I wasn't on the beer last night." We used to play hell with each other. Of course, it was me all the while', Edmonds added, 'but still, I never used to think that.'

86. The Weymouth Echo announces the retirement of Frank Edmonds

Like a Commedia dell'Arte actor, Frank Edmonds played one major role, that of Mr. Punch, throughout his working life. Asked whether his father was buried with any of his puppets in the traditional manner, Nick Edmonds replied, 'I think my father sold his puppets, but to whom I can't remember and he was the only one in the coffin. At least I think so, but you never know, he and Mr. Punch were very close, hand in glove so to speak. He was cremated anyway, the same as he liked his sausages, so we'll never know.'

Curtain Call

'I don't mind, you please yourself. I lead, follow who can!'

Frank Edmonds to recorders of his show

The English seaside holiday comes with its own licence. It offers the freedom to do as you please, whether it's to sunbathe, eat deliciously greasy or sugary foods – battered fish or candyfloss – or bound about in ball games, paddle in the sea, or to potter idly along the sands.

After dark there's a carnival atmosphere amid the thumping music, overflowing pubs and abundant couples: a sudden swinging out of control, like a dizzying fairground ride. Uncrowned, Mr. Punch is the lord of this cheerful misrule, an anarchic figure defying the heavy-handed forces of wedlock, religion and the law; his only friend a clown.

The Punch & Judy show is one of the classic elements of the traditional seaside holiday, although rumour often has it that the show is dying out. Patterns of performance have certainly changed – like the show itself – but this has usually been the way. News of Punch's death has been greatly exaggerated and he is a hard act to kill. While continuing to appear all over the country with his gaudy old street theatre, he still favours the beach. Punch is particularly at home in Weymouth, where he has been entertaining people for over a hundred and thirty years. During fifty of those years he was on the right hand of one puppeteer, Frank Edmonds, professional Punch & Judy man.

It is a sadness that none of Frank Edmonds's children or grandchildren felt able to become Punch & Judy performers, to take up the family tradition of which he was so proud. Yet Edmonds's influence is still felt; his show still goes on.

Punchman Martin Bridle was born and brought up in Weymouth, at a time when Frank Edmonds was a regular part of summer life. He remembers the 'great big crowds' watching his show and how funny it was.

When he attended his first Covent Garden May Fayre commemorating Punch's first appearance in England, Bridle said that he expected performances of a similar standard, which was when 'I realised how good he must have been, because in general I was disappointed'. Bridle joined forces with Rod Burnett, who had spent part of his childhood in Weymouth. Burnett worked the dolls while Martin bottled. To create their show, Martin combined his recollections of Edmonds's performance with aspects of his father's magic act. 'I always conjure up memories of Frank Edmonds on the beach' he said. 'That is the show'.

Vic Banks, who learned his skills from Frank Edmonds as a child – and who worked alongside him in the booth one summer when Frank had injured his arm – remains active as a Punch & Judy man. In the summer of 2011 he gave two shows at the village fete in Cattistock – a place where Frank had performed on a rainy day back in the 1930s. He works with the set of puppets he bought when he was fourteen years old, masking the holes in Punch's well-worn costume with a scatter of sequins. His booth is even older, made by Vic's father about eighty years ago.

87. Vic Banks performing in Cattistock, 2011

On that July Saturday, Vic gave two shows at Cattistock fete, with the first show following Frank's favoured pattern. The play opened with Punch, Judy and the Baby, and the scene ended with Punch killing his wife and child. 'Black Joe from Jamaica' appeared and was frightened by the Crocodile, who proceeded to make a meal of him. Returning, Punch blithely tried to stroke the Crocodile's nose. The Crocodile swallowed not Punch, but his string of sausages, and Punch escaped unharmed. The play was rounded off by Joey, in a rapid echo of an Edmonds performance.

88. Mark Poulton's new booth

Another show goes on in Weymouth – a resort which values its Punch & Judy performers. There is, as always, a dedicated Punchman man on the beach. Professor Mark Poulton performs regularly throughout the season in shows which combine an awareness of the play's history with some surprising innovations.

And that, to give Punch the last few words, is the way to do it.

Tailpiece One
Frank Edmonds's Punch & Judy Script
as remembered by Michael Darrington

As a child I was taken to Weymouth for three or four weeks every year. I became almost obsessed with Frank's Punch & Judy, and would watch all four performances every day. So from the age of about two until I was fourteen (when Frank retired) Punch & Judy on Weymouth beach became my favourite pastime.

SCENE ONE

BOTTLER: Mr. Punch, are you ready?

MR. PUNCH: No.

BOTTLER: Why aren't you ready?

MR. PUNCH: I'm putting on my trousers.

BOTTLER: Well, hurry up. Everyone is waiting to see you.

MR. PUNCH: All right, all right. I'm ready now.

BOTTLER: C'mon then.

MR. PUNCH: All right. Coming up, coming up, coming up, coming up, coming up, coming up, coming up, coming up, coming whaaaaaaaaay. Ooh how'd you do? How'd you do? And how'd you do?

[*Singing and dancing*]

Fiddly diddly dup de diddly di do, fiddly diddly dup de diddly de de. You know, you know, say how you do if you all happy, me all happy too.

BOTTLER: Mr. Punch, how are you?

MR. PUNCH: I'm very well, thank you.

BOTTLER: Shake hands.

MR. PUNCH: Get out of it.

BOTTLER: Ask the boys and girls if they would like to see Judy.

MR. PUNCH: No.

BOTTLER: Why not?

MR. PUNCH: 'Cos I don't want to see her.

BOTTLER: C'mon Mr. Punch. I'm sure the boys and girls want to see her. Don't you boys and girls?

[*Response from the public*]

MR. PUNCH: All right, all right.

[*Mr. Punch then knocks on the 'Pig & Whistle' pub door*]

Judy, my little beauty, come upstairs. Everybody wants to see you.

[*He knocks on the door again*]

C'mon Judy!

[*Judy appears through the window of the pub*]

Ooh, what a pretty face!

[*Judy comes out through the door of the pub*]

What a pretty nose, what a beauty, what a face. C'mon Judy, gimme a kiss.

JUDY: [*Swazzled voice*] What for?

MR. PUNCH: Because I want one.

JUDY: No.

MR. PUNCH: C'mon my little beauty.

JUDY: All right then.

[*Mr. Punch and Judy start kissing with strange swazzled noises, then they start doing a little dance with each other. They accidentally bang the back of their heads together and both end up at the sides of the proscenium*]

MR. PUNCH: Judy, go and get the baby.

JUDY: No.

[*Mr. Punch pushes Judy*]

MR. PUNCH: Go and get him.

[*Judy disappears and reappears with the baby*]

JUDY: Hold the baby.

MR. PUNCH: No, you hold the baby.

[*They throw the baby to each other*]

JUDY: While I go downstairs I want you to teach him to walk.
MR. PUNCH: All right, all right.
[*Judy goes downstairs. Mr. Punch picks up the baby and screams*]
Judy, Judy the baby has no head.
[*Judy reappears*]
JUDY: You're holding him upside down.
[*She turns baby the right way up*]
MR. PUNCH: Get out of it.
[*Mr. Punch knocks Judy downstairs. Mr. Punch tries to teach the baby to walk by saying: Walkie, Walkie, Walkie, but the baby either falls down, walks too slowly, whizzes around too fast or starts crying. Mr. Punch cradles the baby and starts singing*]
MR. PUNCH: 'Go to sleep my baby' … Daddy will hit you if you don't.
[*The baby carries on crying. Mr. Punch sits on the baby. Judy returns*]
JUDY: What are you doing?
MR. PUNCH: I'm babysitting.
JUDY: Give him to me.
MR. PUNCH: No. [Throws baby downstairs, Judy goes downstairs]
That's the way to do it.
[*Judy returns with Mr. Punch's stick and hits him across the back of his head several times while Mr. Punch makes strange noises*]
MR. PUNCH: Give me my stick.
[*Judy hits him again. Mr. Punch grabs one end of the stick and says*]
MR. PUNCH: Give it to me.
JUDY: No.
MR. PUNCH: Give it to me.
JUDY: No.
MR. PUNCH: Won't you give it to me my girl, won't you give it to me?
[*Mr. Punch pushes Judy backwards and forwards against the sides of the proscenium*]
MR. PUNCH: Round and round and round and round.

[*While spinning Judy's body with his stick*]

Won't you give it to me?

[*Mr. Punch knocks Judy on to the playboard and rolls her backwards and forwards*]

Roly-poly. Roly-poly. Roly-poly. Go away Judy, go away.

[*He lifts her with his stick, spins her body around the stick until she falls off downstairs*]

MR. PUNCH: That's the way to do it!

SCENE TWO

[*Voice from downstairs*]

VOICE: That's a terrible thing you have done to Judy, Mr. Punch. Someone is coming that will make you pay for that.

MR. PUNCH: Who is it?

VOICE: You'll soon find out.

MR. PUNCH: Bring him up, bring them all up, I don't care.

[*The Beadle now appears*]

BEADLE: Hi, hi, hi…

[*On the third 'Hi' Mr. Punch hits the Beadle with his stick on to the playboard. The Beadle shakes himself and stands back up*]

BEADLE: Mr. Punch you can't do that.

MR. PUNCH: Why not? [*Hits him with the stick again*]

BEADLE: Don't you know who I am?

MR. PUNCH: No, I don't.

BEADLE: I am the Beadle.

MR. PUNCH: You mean a black beetle?

BEADLE: No, I don't mean a black beetle. I am a sort of policeman.

MR. PUNCH: You mean a postman?

BEADLE: No, I don't mean a postman.

MR. PUNCH: Well, who are you then?

BEADLE: I'm an officer of the law and I'm here to take you down.

MR. PUNCH: And I'm here to knock you down. [*Hits Beadle again with his stick*]

BEADLE: Give me your stick.

MR. PUNCH: Here [*Hits him again. Beadle pushes Mr. Punch*] Don't you push me!

[*Pushes him back. They push each other backwards and forwards three times, then they start hitting each other*]

BEADLE: That's a topper.

MR. PUNCH: That's a whopper.

BEADLE: That's a good 'un.

MR. PUNCH: That's a better one.

BEADLE: You.

MR. PUNCH: You.

BEADLE: Me.

MR. PUNCH: Me. [*Mr. Punch hits Beadle downstairs with his stick*] I don't care for nobody. That's the way to do it. I don't care.

[*Mr. Punch sits on playboard and starts singing*]

Oh, I do like to be beside the seaside …

SCENE THREE

[*While Mr. Punch is singing, Joey the Clown pops up and down blowing raspberries and saying 'cuckoo'. Mr. Punch keeps turning around looking to see who is making the noises. Mr. Punch looking downstairs says*]

MR. PUNCH: Who is it?

[*From downstairs*]

JOEY: It's Joey.

MR. PUNCH: Joey?

[*Joey pops up into Mr. Punch's face, saying:*]

JOEY: Helloee. Hello Mr. Punch. How are you?

MR. PUNCH: I'm very well.

JOEY: Well shake hands.

MR. PUNCH: All right.

[*They go to shake hands. Joey grabs Punch's stick and hits him with it*]

Ouuu … What did you do that for?

JOEY: … What did I do that for? Because you're doing it to everybody else. I won't do it again. C'mon, shake hands.

MR. PUNCH: No, you'll hurt me.

JOEY: I won't hurt you. I won't hurt him, will I boys and girls?

MR. PUNCH: All right, all right. C'mon then.

[*They go to shake hands again. Once more Joey hits Punch with the stick*] You said you wouldn't hurt me.

JOEY: All right, you know what I'm going to do? I'm going to let you hit me.

MR. PUNCH: Oh all right then.

JOEY: I'm going to lay my head down over here. [*Taps the playboard with his hand*]

And on the count of three you can hit me with your stick. All right?

MR. PUNCH: All right.

JOEY: Here we go then. [*Lays down on the playboard*]

Start counting.

[*Mr. Punch holds stick over Joey's head and counts 'one'. Joey repeats after Punch*]

MR. PUNCH: One.

JOEY: One and a half.

MR. PUNCH: Two.

JOEY: Two and a half.

MR. PUNCH: Three. [*Goes to hit Joey. Joey slides along the playboard and Punch misses him*]

Oh, you moved. Come here.

[*He picks Joey up and moves him to his original spot. This goes on several times until Joey grabs the stick and hits Mr. Punch. Mr. Punch chases him around the stage until Joey finally hides under the playboard at the front of the booth*]

Where are you?

JOEY: I'm over here. [*Punch looks over the playboard and says*]

MR. PUNCH: Where?

JOEY: Here. [*Hits Punch in the face*]

MR. PUNCH: Oh dear, oh dear, oh dear …

[*From under the playboard Joey starts singing a rhyme*]

JOEY: Around the town …

MR. PUNCH: What?

JOEY: Tuppence a pound …

MR. PUNCH: What?

JOEY: A penny …

MR. PUNCH: A what?

JOEY: A lump.

[*Hits Punch again. Joey comes out from under the playboard and hits Punch with his stick. Punch grabs the stick and chases Joey all around the stage again until Joey hits him on the nose and disappears downstairs*]

SCENE FOUR

[*Mr. Punch sits on the playboard and says*]

MR. PUNCH: Oh dear, oh dear. My poor nose. What a pity. What a pity.

VOICE: Never mind Mr. Punch. You sit up there and enjoy yourself.

MR. PUNCH: I will my boy, I will.

[*Mr. Punch starts singing again. As he sings the Crocodile slowly appears. Punch continues singing and moving from side to side. Without Punch realising, the Crocodile keeps trying to bite Punch's hand, which it eventually does*]

MR. PUNCH: [*Screams out*] Ouuu. [*Slides to the side of the stage, trembling*]

What is it? What is it?

VOICE: Surely you know what it is.

MR. PUNCH: No I don't.

VOICE: It's a Crocodile.

MR. PUNCH: [*With trembling voice*] Oh.

[*Mr. Punch starts talking to the Crocodile and attempting to stroke it*]

Come here, come here. There's a good boy. There's a good

boy.

[*He strokes the Crocodile from his eyes to his nose and back several times. On the third stroke the Crocodile quickly opens his mouth and tries to bite Punch's hand again. This happens several times. Punch then grabs his stick and says*]

I know what. [*He hits the Crocodile several times, saying*]

There, there, there…I know. [*He taps Crocodile's mouth*]

C'mon! Open up, open up…

[*Punch pushes his stick into Crocodile's mouth. Crocodile starts swallowing stick while Mr. Punch says*]

Look at him, look at him, look at him…You've swallowed my stick. Give it back. C'mon, open up.

[*Crocodile opens his mouth and Punch sees a string of sausages inside*]

Oh…

[*Mr. Punch tries to grab sausages from Crocodile's mouth. Both Punch and Crocodile go around the stage until Punch has finally got all the sausages. Punch sits on the playboard and starts singing*]

Fi di de di do singing hotdogs for tea, hotdogs for tea, hotdogs for tea.

[*Swinging sausages in his hand. Crocodile tries to grab sausages back and a struggle ensues. Crocodile eventually grabs Punch by the nose. Punch says*]

Ouuu me nose, ouuu me nose. [*Punch disappears downstairs*]

SCENE FIVE

[*While Crocodile remains on the playboard, Mr. Crow comes up dancing and singing*]

MR. CROW: Oh, oh, Antonio, she's gone away, she left me on my ownio, all on my ownio.

[*Realising he has got an audience Mr. Crow stops singing and starts talking to the audience*]

Oh, hello. How are you? Are you all having a lovely time? Well I don't suppose any of you know who I am, do you? Well, my name is Mr. Crow, Mr. C.R.O.W. Crow. That's the way you spell it.

Now when I say 'hello boys and girls' I want you all to shout back as loud as you can 'Hello Mr. Crow'. Have you got it? Here we go then. Hello boys and girls.

[*The audience responds*]

No, no, no…. I could hardly hear you. I want you to shout much louder than that. Well, try again. Hello boys and girls.

[*Audience responds much louder*]

Ha, ha, ha, that's much better. Well there is quite a lot of you here today. [*Looks right*]

There's a lot of you over there. [*Looking forward*]

and a lot of you there.

[*He goes to say the same thing looking to the left and comes face to face with the Crocodile*]

Oh, hello.

[*Crocodile and Mr. Crow look each other up and down and side to side. Mr. Crow turns back to the audience and asks*]

What on earth is it?

[*Audience responds*]

AUDIENCE: It's a crocodile!

MR. CROW: It's a what?

AUDIENCE: It's a crocodile!

MR. CROW: Oh, it's a crokee okee okeedile, is it?

[*He laughs hysterically, banging his head on the playboard and proscenium*]

What does a crocodile do?

AUDIENCE: It bites you!

MR. CROW: It what?

AUDIENCE: It bites you! [*Mr. Crow laughs again*]

MR. CROW: It won't bite me. No, no, no. It likes me. [*Talking to the Crocodile*]

You like me, don't you? [*Crocodile nods*]

You won't bite me, will you? [*Crocodile nods again*]

[*Laughing*] No, no, no, you won't bite me, will you?

[*Crocodile shakes his head. Mr. Crow turns to the audience*]

I told you he won't bite me. Do you know what I'm going to do?

I am going to sit right up there.

[*Mr. Crow touches Crocodile on his head. He sits on the head and says*]

Oh, it's lovely up here. I can see you all much better now.

[*The Crocodile lifts his head and Mr. Crow slides down his nose on to the playboard. Mr. Crow says*]

I like that. I think I'll give it another go.

[*And does so several times. Tapping on the Crocodile's mouth, he says*]

Show us your teeth. [*Crocodile shakes his head*]

Don't be shy. Show everyone your nice white teeth.

[*Crocodile quickly opens his mouth and swings his head over the playboard*]

Look at that. Hasn't he got lovely teeth and a lovely red tongue?

Do you know what I'm going to do? I'm going to stroke his tongue.

[*Speaks to Crocodile*]

C'mon, open up again.

[*Mr. Crow starts to stroke Crocodile's tongue and says*]

There…look at that. He won't bite me.

[*At which point the Crocodile attempts to bite Mr. Crow's hand. Mr. Crow jumps back*]

Oh dear…I know what I'll do. I'll give him my wooden leg to bite, because if he bites that it won't hurt me.

[*Mr. Crow holds up his wooden leg and says*]

Here we go then.

[*He teases the Crocodile by pulling his wooden leg away every time the Crocodile snaps his mouth. Eventually the Crocodile grabs Mr. Crow's good leg and spins around the stage with him while Mr. Crow screams*]

Aaaaaghhhh…

[*The Crocodile carries him downstairs*]

SCENE SIX

[*Mr. Punch reappears*]

MR. PUNCH: Oh dear, oh dear. What a pity, what a pity, what a pity. Never mind, never mind.

VOICE: You carry on enjoying yourself Mr. Punch.

MR. PUNCH: I will, Master. I will.

[*Mr. Punch starts singing again. From behind Punch appears the Bogey Man (Devil) making a strange whirring sound. Punch turns round and the Bogey Man disappears. Punch carries on singing but it happens again*]

MR. PUNCH: What was it? What was it?

VOICE: That's the Bogey Man.

MR. PUNCH: It's a what?

VOICE: The Bogey Man.

MR. PUNCH: What does he want?

VOICE: He's come to take you down.

MR. PUNCH: What for?

VOICE: 'Cos he thinks you were very bad.

MR. PUNCH: Well bring him up. I don't care for no Bogey Man.

[*At which point the Bogey Man reappears behind Punch, still making strange noises. The Bogey Man disappears and reappears in several places including the 'Pig and Whistle' pub, under the playboard and frantically all around the stage. Punch keeps trying to hit him but misses every time until finally he pins the Bogey Man against the side of the proscenium and says*]

I'm not scared of no Bogey Man. Go away.

[*The Bogey Man and Punch fight backwards and forwards with the stick until Punch finally hits the Bogey Man on to the playboard*]

Here we go my boy. Roly-poly, roly-poly, roly-poly.

[*Punch rolls him along the stage with his stick. He picks up the Bogey Man with his stick and spins him around with it until the Bogey Man falls off downstairs*]

Go away Bogey Man. Go away.

FINAL SCENE

[*Joey pops back up*]
JOEY: What's been going on up here then?
MR. PUNCH: I killed the Bogey Man.
JOEY: You can't kill the Bogey Man.
MR. PUNCH: Well I did. [*Joey sees the evidence*]
JOEY: Did he kill the Bogey Man?
AUDIENCE:Yes!
JOEY: Well that's the first good thing you've done. So I think it's time to go now. So say goodbye to everyone.
[*Punch & Joey bow to the audience three times*]
MR. PUNCH: How d'you do, how d'you do and how d'you do…
[*They both disappear downstairs. End of show*]

Note: This was the basic routine of the show, but Frank would add different extras: the Chinese Plate-Spinners; the Boxers; the Doctor; the Hangman; the Ghost, the Policeman; the counting routine, the spider routine and the punchball. He also used to have a hanging routine and a part where the baby was thrown into the audience, but he stopped doing these in the middle of the 1960s.

Tailpiece Two
Parlaree

This glossary has been selected from two lexigraphical works by Eric Partridge, *A Dictionary of the Underworld* and *Here, There and Everywhere*, with additional material from Henry Mayhew's *London Labour and the London Poor* and Robert Leach's *The Punch & Judy Show*. It does not claim to be comprehensive as this would not be possible, but it does give some sense of the individuality and vigour of the tongue.

Among the many thousands of entries in Partridge's *Dictionary of the Underworld* are words used by (among others) convicts, racketeers, crooks, beggars, tramps, white-slave traders, drug-traffickers and spivs. The vocabulary of palaree which survives seems to suggest that, unlike most of these people, showmen stayed mainly on the right side of the law – if not of the sheets.

The majority of the words derive from Italian, others come from Romany, Yiddish or various cants; while the remainder have obscure derivations. Spellings are variable and phonetic: parlaree was never a written language. Even its name is spelt in several different ways.

Some of the terms, like the first and second in the list, have passed into colloquial English.

barney – a mob (specifically used by Punch & Judy men)
beve – Ital. *bevere* – drink
bevey omi – drunkard
bionc, beong – Ital. *bianco*, white – a shilling or other silver coin
bivvy – Ital. *bevere* – to drink – beer; shant of bivvy, a pot or quart of beer (Mayhew)
bonar – Ital. *buono* – good
bona parlare – language, name of patter (Mayhew)
borarco – Spanish *barracho* – drunkard
buffer – dog (1610)

buvare – liquor

caroon – Ital. *corona* – crown piece (five shillings). [Romany kroona]

carsey – Ital. *casa* – house

catever, kartever – Ital. *cativa*, bad – bad or inferior, hence shady

catever cartzo – Ital. *cazzo* – syphilis

chaffer – tongue (low slang)

chaffering homa Ital. *uomo chichiarante*(?)

charpering omi – Ital. *cercare*, to search – policeman

charpering carsey – police station

chauvering – Romany *charva*, to touch, meddle with – sexual intercourse

chauvering dona – a prostitute

chavvies – Romany *charvo* – children

chinker – Ital. *cinque* – five

chinker saltee – five pence

clod – penny, copper coin

co & co – partner (Mayhew). Ital. *questa questa*

dacha – Ital. *dieci* – ten

deaner – Yiddish *dinoh* – coin, shilling

dinarly – Ital. *denaro* – money (small coin). Nantee dinarly – no money

dona – Ital. *donna* – woman

dooe, doee – Ital. *due* – two

Eine – London

feelies – children

fielia – Ital. *figlia* – daughter, girl

gajo – Romany – outsider

ham – a loafer

hambone – bad showman. One who 'flobs' his figures – lets them droop

hedge – hedge and ditch – pitch (20thC.)

joggering omi – street musician. From Ital. *giocare* –to play, sport, jest

letty – Ital. *letto* – sleep, bed

letties – lodgings. nanti parlare, scarper de letti – shut your mouth, leave the lodgings

madza, medzies – Ital. *mezzo* – half. Especially madza caroon – half a crown, madza poona – half a sovereign, madza saltee, a halfpenny

manjaree, mungarly – Ital. *mangiare* – to eat – bread, food

mungarly casa – a baker's shop

mozzy – Ital. *moglia* – wife: hence Judy

multy – Ital. *molto* – much

nantee, nanty, nunty – Ital. *niente* – nothing – not any

nante dinarly – no money

nanti menzies – (pronounced 'majjies') Ital. *mezzo* – half, half a crown – no money, penniless

nanti parlaver – stop talking! hold your tongue!

nobba – Ital. *nove* – nine

nobby slum – collecting bag

omi (homa) – Ital. *uomo* – a man

omi of the carsey – landlord

oney – Italianisation of the English 'one' – Ital. *uno*

orderly – quickly

ordinare – Ital. *ordinare* – give orders

paloney, pollone – Ital. *pollone* – young woman (lit. a tender shoot)

parker – Ital. *partire* – leave – pay up, parker with or from dinarly

parker, parkey – to part, give.

parlaree, parlyaree, parlary – Ital. *parlare* – to speak. 'Language of circus-men, showmen and itinerant or low actors; based on Italian, and to some extent on Lingua Franca, it was common in England c.1850, though it existed much earlier.' (Eric Partridge)

parney, parnee, pani – Romany, ex-Hindustani – rain

pipares – pipes

ponging – used by Dickens in *Hard Times*: 'Loose in his ponging' (Bad in his tumbling)

ponte – Ital. *pondo* – pound

poona – pound sterling, probably by analogy with corona

poove, pooving – food, feeding

professor – Ital. *professore* – honorary title of Punch & Judy men

quartereen – a farthing (a quarter of a penny)

quarterer – Ital. *quattro* – four

questa questa – partner

rise (or raise) a barney – to collect a mob. 'A term used by patterers and swassle-box'

salta, saltee (pl. saltre) – Ital. *soldo* (pl. *soldi*) – penny

saulty – penny

say – Ital. *sei* – six

scarper – Ital. *scappare* – to flee, escape. There is a stock character in the Commedia dell'Arte called Scapino.

schwassle box – Yiddish ex-German *schwatsen* – to chatter – hence, chatter-box

sharping omee – policeman

slang – a travelling show, a performance (Mayhew)

slanging – performing, exhibiting in fairs or markets

slum – call, or unknown tongue (Mayhew)

slum/slumareys – Rom *slummery* – figure, frame, scenes, properties

fake the slum – swindle

slum fake – the coffin in which the hangman is removed

snow – silver coin

suppelar – a hat

swatchel – swazzle – Mr. Punch.

swatchel cove – a chattering fellow. Man who gives a Punch & Judy performance

tambora – Ital. *tamburo* – drum (Mayhew)

tober – Irish Gypsy – the road

trey – Ital. *tre* – three

ultra cattiva – Ital. *molto cattiva* – very bad

una soldi – Ital. *uno soldo* – one penny

vardo – Romany *wagon* – caravan

vedring – Ital. *vedere*, to see – Romany *vater* – to watch

Questa homa a vadring the slum, scarper it. Orderly. There's someone looking at the slum, be off quickly

yeute – none, no`

Counting

Eric Partridge gives these numbers as specific to Punch & Judy showmen.
They are derived from Italian.

1. una
2. due
3. tre
4. quatto
5. chickwa
6. sei
7. sette
8. oddo
9. novo
10. deger
11. long deger

Say, sei can be used in combination with numbers 1-5. e.g. say oney saltee
is seven pence; say dooe saltee is eight pence and so on.

Tailpiece Three
Punch & Judy: its origins, history and significance

by

Revd. Glanville T. Magor

Origins

The old Attic Comedy of Ancient Greece was political.
The poets ridiculed contemporary politicians and events.
The plays were masked and one actor played the main role.
Three or four other actors played all the remaining parts, changing masks
to reappear as different characters, apart from the Chorus under its leader.
Most plays were based upon confrontations with the main character, lead-
ing to the discomforting of his opponents.
The plays changed over the centuries and influenced other drama for sim-
ilar farces appeared in southern Italy.

The Atellan Farces

The farces in southern Italy were also anti-establishment.
They involved a larger speaking cast than in Greece with stock characters
and clowns.
The actors remained masked and included females.
Over the centuries a number of stock characters emerged.
During the Christian era the plays incurred the wrath of the Church for
immorality, nude actresses and attacks on it.
Around 560 A.D. the Church persuaded the Emperor Justinian to ban

drama – this ban lasted 900 years in Europe during which time nothing like our drama existed.

1453 A.D.

The crucial date for modern civilisation was when the Muslims came West, through Asia Minor into Europe.

The early Christian Church had deliberately destroyed all traces of Greek culture which it could find as it was 'pagan' and therefore evil.

Christian Europe believed the biblical flat plate and bowl version of the world, even though the Greeks had known that the earth was spherical and had calculated its size and weight.

While Christian Europe was in the 'Dark Ages', the Muslims had brilliant civilisations, south of the Sahara as well as in Arab lands, built on what Greek knowledge they had salvaged and translated into Arabic.

In 1453, with the Fall of Constantinople, this knowledge burst into Europe, through Italy, and gave us the Renaissance, freeing Science from the Church and enabling the development of modern civilisation.

The commedia dell'arte

At the Renaissance some Italians sought to revive Greek drama – the tragedies failed but the comedies succeeded.

These comedies were masked and centred on Pantalone and his friends, supported and frustrated by a host of clowns who ensured that the play ended happily, for the lover and the lass – who, with the maid, did not wear masks.

Every play was 'improvised' but, as the actors always played the same roles, much of the dialogue and 'business' was from memory, fitted into a new outline for each play.

The plays were brilliantly performed and reached France.

One of the clowns was a vulgar hunchback – Pulicianella

.

Other sources

The Punch play developed by weaving together elements from three traditions, THE GREEK-ITALIAN FARCES and the two following:

THE MIRACLE PLAYS These popular dramas gave us stock characters such as Mrs. Noah and themes such as the defeat of the devil. Judy is Mrs. Noah reborn and genuine Punch & Judy plays end with Punch killing the devil.

THE JESTER TRADITION Jesters ended up as 'Merry Andrews' in the fairs – hunchbacked, with pot belly, ruff, big buttons and slapstick – all found on the traditional Punch. He always wears the red and yellow motley costume of the traditional jester.

From Italy to England

The Italian Players established themselves in Paris – with difficulty – but eventually the demand for French dialogue led to written scripts and the improvisation ceased.

Some Italians came to London but objection to actresses led to them being 'pippin pelted' and rejected.

Some Commedia characters entered fairground life, both actors and puppets (the Commonwealth tolerated puppets).

At the Restoration an Italian puppeteer, Signor Bologna, presented plays at Covent Garden and, on May 9th 1662, Pepys saw these plays and liked the character, Pollichinella – a white costumed clown with a black hook-nosed mask.

Punch the String Puppet

The Italian name was quickly shortened to Punch, who had come to England as a string puppet (Marionette).

Signor Bologna (real name Pietro Gimonde) played before Charles II and was given a gold chain and a medal worth £25.

Others played Punch at Bath, Bristol and Covent Garden and he acquired an English wife – Joan.

The 17th century puppet plays became very refined and the intrusion of the vulgar Punch was increasingly disliked by the intellectuals, though not by the common people.

Partly due to the difficulties of using string puppts Punch declined in the eighteenth century and almost died out.

Punch redivivus

About 1780 another Italian puppeteer, called Piccini, used glove puppets to revive the Punch show using a 'fit-up' similar to those of the present time.

From the last two decades of the 1700s and the first two of the 1800s there are many illustrations of Punch shows.

Punch is loud-mouthed and Judy is aggressive. Other characters appeared who quickly vanished from the play.

The little drama quickly acquired characteristics from many centuries before, being a play which viewed society from the point of view of the common man, mocking authority and pretentiousness.

Social Background

18th and early 19th century society was very different from ours, reflected in the themes of the Punch drama.

Power was centred in the landed gentry who controlled Parliament and, through Magistrates and Vestrymen, local politics, supported by the clergy of the Established Church.

Hanging was the punishment for 400 crimes and for those who stole anything worth more than 6d and ran away.

The common people had neither voice nor vote.

In France they guillotined their 'betters' – in England they laughed at them through the Punch & Judy show.

Essential Elements

As in the Attic comedies, those with power or position were the targets. Most shows included a domestic conflict and a conflict with those in political or religious authority. From early days political figures appeared in shows or in cartoons based upon Punch & Judy. The magazine PUNCH was so called because its intention was to be satirical and anti-establishment.

Although scripts exist of shows from the mid-nineteenth century there was no set formula for the show. Then, as now, quality and approach varied. Two secondary authority figures, the Officer and the Beadle, appear and usually are dealt with by Punch, as is the supreme example of the power of Society – the Hangman. In various shows Punch ridicules the FAMILY, the GENTRY and HELL-FIRE RELIGION – the three pillars of respectable society in 18th & 19th century England.

Change and Decay

The Victorian period saw great changes in the attitude to leisure – many of the Fairs and Holidays were abolished or curtailed.

Those who had earned their living in the greatly extended fairs had to find new sources of income – the Punch man became a street player.

A 'pitch' under a rich person's window could lead to being invited inside for a command performance (Short & Codlin in Dickens's *Old Curiosity Shop*).

This led to a fundamental change – what had been an anti-establishment play for adults was now changed for very practical reasons to one suitable for showing in the parlour when children were present.

The political element was suppressed and remained so until about three decades ago. The plays were 'padded out' with boxers or clowns.

Today, in spite of PC objections, many seem to consider the play suitable for very young children, so puppeteers tend to throw political jokes over them to adults at the back of the crowd.

A Traditional Show

INTRODUCTION Joey the Clown, Toby Dog (now a puppet), Crocodile and sausages.

ACT 1 THE FAMILY Two triangles: Punch, Judy & Baby. Punch, Judy & Pretty Polly (mistress – Polly Peachum from *Beggar's Opera*) ending with Punch turning on the aggressive Judy and killing her.

ACT 2 THE GENTRY characters such as Doctor or Mayor with Policeman, Beadle, Hangman, Lord Chief Justice – ending with Punch tricking the Hangman.

ACT 3 HELL-FIRE RELIGION Parson, Ghost of Judy, Devil.

CONCLUSION Fight with killing of the Devil

.

The Traditional Punch Cast

Punch, Judy, Baby, Pretty Polly, Joey the Clown, Toby Dog, Crocodile, Hector the Horse.

Doctor, Mayor, Policeman, Beadle, Judge, Hangman.

Parson, Ghost of Judy, Devil.

Blackman, Blindman, Courtier, Scaramouch (These now are rarely seen.) With the exception of the Crocodile (19th century) all these characters have been in the show for two hundred years.

Various others have disappeared such as the Publican, Undertakers, Sailor, Mr. Jones (Toby's owner) and contemporary political characters etc.

Acknowledgements

Thanks for their help in the making of this book go to Maureen Attwooll, Vic Banks, Sylvester Bone, Martin Bridle, David Brown, Michael Darrington, Ray DaSilva, Alison & Brian Davey, Val Dicker, Frank Edmonds, Nick Edmonds, Keith Ellis, Geoff Felix, Mark Forrest, Dawn Gould, Fred Hawkins, David Haysom, Crystal Johnson, Glanville Magor, Elsie Marshall, Sheila Milton, Stephen Milverton, Frances Nicholson, Silvia Noakes, Mick Orr, Ted Parker, Mark Poulton, Joy Rodber, Reg & David Saville, John Styles and Margaret Wyllie

Bridport History Centre, the British Library, St. Pancras & Colindale, Dorset History Centre, Leeds Central Reference Library, Swanage Museum, Martin Ayres and the staff of Swanage Town Hall, Weymouth Reference Library, Theatre Archive, Victoria & Albert Museum, Yeovil Reference Library

ILLUSTRATIONS

Front cover, Robert Leach; frontispiece 2, 3, 12, 23, 38, 40, 41, 59, 63, 66, 81, 82, 83, 85, 86, Frank Edmonds (grandson); frontispiece, 5, 16, 17, 24, 65; Roy Tomlinson; 7, 45, 46, 47, 48 Swanage Town Hall; 18, 25, 27, 87, Mick Orr; 19, Geoff Felix; 22, Portland Museum; 28, Nick Edmonds; 29, Sylvester Bone; 26, 31, Dorset County Museum; 32, 37, Barry Cuff; 33, 34, 35, Weymouth Reference Library; 36, 88, Mark Poulton; 42, 51, 53, Swanage Museum; 43, Tate Gallery; 44, Christopher Milverton; 49, Philip Oakes; 27, Peter Brough; 52, David Brown; 58, Wendy Wharam; 60, Keith Ellis; 64, Michael Darrington; 67, *Dorset Life*; 68, 69, Glanville Magor; 70, 71, Brian and Alison Davey; 72, 73, 74, Joy Rodber; 84, John Styles

Every attempt has been made to trace the copyright holders. Any omissions will be corrected in future editions.

Bibliography

ENTRANCES:

MUCH OF THE INFORMATION about Frank Edmonds's early life was supplied by Frank's grandson Frank and his son Nick, who supplied me with many well-researched and lively pieces (and several rounds of drinks). I could not have written the book without their help in this and the following chapters. Other material came from Robert Leach's definitive *The Punch & Judy Show* (Batsford,1985) and his essay 'The Swatchel Omi: Punch and Judy and the Oral Tradition' (*Theatre Quarterly*, vol.ix, Winter 1980). These sources have been used throughout the text.

Byrom, Michael, *Punch and Judy: its origins and evolution*, DaSilva Puppet Books, 1988

Kelly's Directories, Weymouth, 1932–33, 1936–37, 1938–39, 1940–41

Mayhew, Henry. London *Labour and the London Poor*, 1851

Pepys, Samuel. *Diaries of Samuel Pepys*, Vol. III, 1662, Bell & Hyman 1970

Taylor, Vic. *Reminiscences of a Showman*, Allen Lane, 1971

Whanslaw, H. W. *Everybody's Marionette Book*, Wells Gardner, Darton and Co. [1935]

Wilkinson, Walter. *The Peep Show*, Geoffrey Bles, 1927

Wilkinson, Walter, *Puppets through Lancashire*, Geoffrey Bles, 1936

Dorset Echo, April 21 2004

Felix, Geoff. 'A New Light on Piccini', Punch & Judy Fellowship, May Fayre, 2006

Undated article in *Southern Times*, 'Punch and Judy Still Popular', [1934]

Minute Books of Swanage Urban District Council, 1930s

Minute Books of Weymouth Corporation's Pavilion Garden and Amusement Committee (Dorset History Centre:AD7/13/1–17)

GOLDEN DAYS: THE 1930S

Weymouth Corporation's Beach and Entertainments Committee's Minute Books at Dorset History Centre (AD7/13/) provided much of the information on beach life in this chapter. The *Southern Times* interview with Edmonds in 1934 was also very useful.

Matheson, Rosa. *Trip: the annual holiday of GWR's Swindon Works*, Tempus, 2000

Powys, John Cowper. *The Dorset Year*, Powys Press, 1998

Townsend, Kay. *A Showman's Story*, 2006

Walton, John K. *The British Seaside. Holidays and resorts in the twentieth century*, Manchester University Press, 2000

Weymouth Corporation's Official Guides, 1920s, 1930s

Dorset Echo, 'Weymouth's Swindon Day', July 9 1965

Southern Times, 'Memorable Day for Weymouth', July 22 1939; '50,000 Give Tumultuous Welcome to Royal Family', July 29 1939. (With thanks to Maureen Attwooll for discovering these two articles.)

V & A Theatre Archive, Gerald Morice Collection, box 187: letter from Will Hayward to Gerald Morice, August 1955; box 191: letters from Frank Edmonds to Gerald Morice, 20/2/1939, 26/5/1939; box 24: 6/6/1940 Geoff Felix, performer and archivist of Punch, kindly provided a list of some the contents of the box files in the Collection. I'm grateful for this and all his other help – and for his patience with my endless questions.

INTERLUDE

Recollections of Sheila Milton, Weymouth resident who lived in the town throughout the Second World War. Edmonds family memories, supplied by Frank and Nick Edmonds.

Attwooll, Maureen, *Bumper Book of Weymouth*, Halsgrove, 2006

Attwooll, Maureen, *Second Bumper Book of Weymouth*, Dorset Books, 2009

Attwooll, Maureen & Harrison, Denise, *Weymouth and Portland at War*, Dovecote Press, 1993

AFTER THE WAR

Vic Banks provided a vivid description of an Edmonds show, from the viewpoint of a performer. Michael Darrington, whose memories of Frank Edmonds's show (and script) appear in later chapters, was the obliging source of much of the information on Fred Darrington.

Bone, Stephen. *British Weather*, Collins, 1946
Cox, Ian. *The South Bank Exhibition*, HMSO, 1951
Liebling, A. J. *Normandy Revisited*, Simon & Schuster, 1958
Manning, Rosemary. *Corridor of Mirrors*, Women's Press, 1987
Page, Edward. *A Weymouth Childhood in the 1950s*, Amberley, 2010
Weymouth Echo, 'Where Weymouth Leads', July 21 1945
World's Fair, January 25 1947
Minute Books of Weymouth Corporation's Beach and Entertainments Committee, op.cit.
Unattributed article 'The Happy Sandman', August 28 1983, Weymouth Reference Library

SWANAGE: DREAMS AMD NIGHTMARES

David Haysom, Curator of Swanage Museum, was an invaluable source of information for this chapter. The Minute Books of Swanage Urban District, in Swanage Town Hall and Swanage Museum, contain a fascinating assortment of material on Punch & Judy men. Christopher Milverton was a generous provider of information on Ernest Brisbane.

Binzen, Bill. *Punch and Jonathan*, Macmillan, 1970
Denton, Pennie, *Seaside Surrealism*: Paul Nash in Swanage, Peveril Press, 2002
Eates, Margot. *Paul Nash 1889–1946*, John Murray, 1973
Fisher, John. *Tony Hancock: the definitive biography*, Futura, 2009
Harris, Alexandra. *Romantic Moderns*, Thames & Hudson, 2010
James, M. R. *More Ghost Stories of an Antiquary*, 1911
Lewer, David & Smale, Dennis. *Swanage Past*, Phillimore, 1994
Nash, Paul. *Fertile Image*, Faber, 1951

Oakes, Philip. *Tony Hancock*, Woburn-Futura, 1975

'Petition on behalf of Professor T. Day' [1904], Swanage Museum

Purbeck Independent, December 5 1996

Swanage & Wareham Guardian, September 10 & 17, 1904

V & A Theatre Archive, Gerald Morice Collection, box 35: letter from Percy Press to Gerald Morice, 4/11/1962

PUPPETS ON A STRING

Mark Poulton, expert on Punch & Judy booths, helpfully explained some of the practicalities of marionette shows.

Bablet, Denis. *Edward Gordon Craig*, Heinemann, 1966

Craig, Edward Gordon. 'The Actor and the Über-Marionette', The Mask, April 1908

Felix, Geoff (ed.) *Conversations With Punch*, Geoff Felix, 1994

Leeper, Janet. *Edward Gordon Craig Designs for the Theatre*, Penguin, 1948

Speaight, George. *History of the English Puppet Theatre*, Southern Illinois University Press, 1990 (second edition)

Walton, John K. *The British Seaside. Holidays and resorts in the twentieth century*, op.cit.

Whanslaw, H. W. *Everybody's Marionette Book*, op.cit

Milsom, Pete. 'Memories of Frank Edmonds. A rare audio interview with Weymouth's longest serving Punch & Judy man', Punch & Judy Fellowship CD, [1967]

Weymouth Echo, 'There's Magic Still in Punch and Judy', August 14 1959

V & A Theatre Archive, Gerald Morice Collection, box 191: letters from Frank Edmonds to Gerald Morice, 26/5/1939; box 24: 16/6/1940; box 176: Percy Press to Gerald Morice, 4/10/1968

LYME BAY

Unperturbed by my unsociably early arrival at their house, Alison and Brian Davey were most hospitable and helpful. I also spent an entertaining and informative morning with Glanville Magor and another with Mrs. Joy Rodber.

TRADE SECRETS

I am very grateful to Michael Darrington for transcribing Frank Ed-monds's play from his childhood memories of the show in the 1960s–1970s.

Collier, John Payne (ed.) *The Tragical Comedy, or Comical Tragedy, of Punch and Judy*, S. Prowett, 1828

Edwards, Glyn. *Successful Punch & Judy*, DaSilva Puppet Books, 2000

Mayhew, Henry. *London Labour and the London Poor*, op.cit.

Partridge, Eric. *Here, There and Everywhere, essays on language*, Hamish Hamilton, 1950

Smith of London, Professor. *The Book of Punch & Judy*, Hamley Bros., 1906

Stead, Philip John. *Mr. Punch*, Evans Brothers, 1950

Woodensconce, Papernose. *The Wonderful Drama of Punch and Judy*, DaSilva Puppet Books, 2001

Pall Mall Gazette, June 15 1887

Strand Magazine, vol. X, June– December 1895

Weymouth Echo, August 14 1959, op.cit.; 'After 50 years "the Punch man" is still thrilled by children's laughter', June 23 1962

William Marwood; www.billgreenwell.com/lost_lives

THE END OF THE SHOW?

Andrews, M. *O Little Filey!* 1948

Dorset Evening Echo, 'Weymouth Punch and Judy man dies', June 2 1964; 'The show goes on and never loses popularity', July 14 1966; 'Punch and Judy man to care for crash orphans', September 14 1966; 'Can it be the end? October 1 1968; 'What a pity, it's goodbye children for Weymouth's Mr. Punch', January 19 1976

World's Fair, October 3 1981

V & A Theatre Archive, Gerald Morice Collection, box 176: Percy Press to Gerald Morice, 4/10/1968

CURTAIN CALL

Vic Banks gave me many useful insights into his Cattistock show.
Felix, Geoff (ed.) *Conversations with Punch*, op.cit.

Last – but not least – I would like to thank Frances Nicholson for her careful scrutiny of the typescript of this book.

Index